Rodney The Cat
Legacy Edition

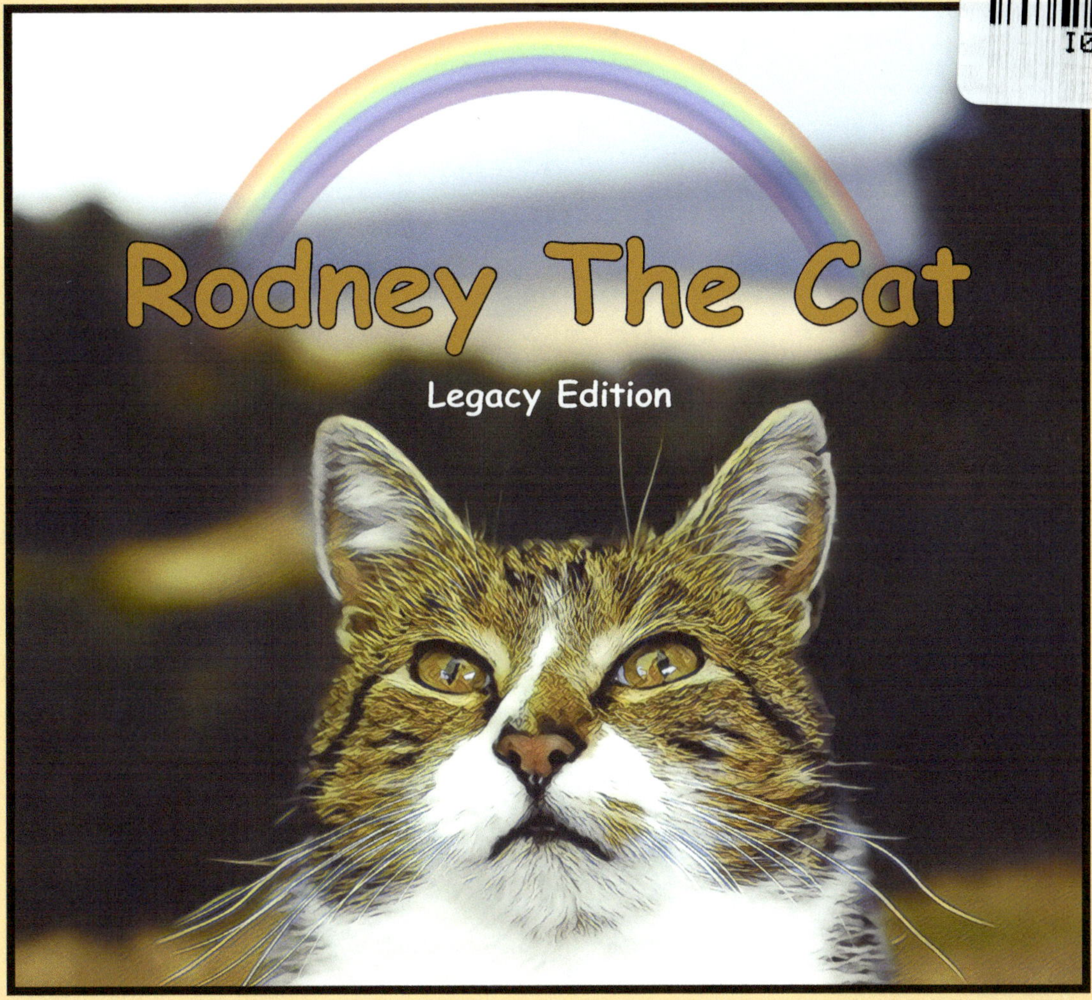

Published by **Rodney The Cat World Famous In New Zealand** ™

Copyright 2023 **Rodney The Cat World Famous In New Zealand** ™

ALL RIGHTS RESERVED
No part of this publication may be reproduced, stored in a retrieval system transmitted in any form or by any means, electronic, mechanical, photocopying, recording or otherwise, without prior written permission from the publisher.

ISBN 978-1-7385812-4-5

Although inspired by real animals, people and events, this story is a work of fiction.

Preface: 16 June 2020

"Just dump him somewhere. Lazy little sod! I'm so damned sick and tired of him! Hair all over the counter… footprints on the stock."

"What? Seriously? Rodney is *our cat*, Dude! He's *used* to people feeding him and caring for…"

"He's *just a bloody cat,* dammit! He can take care of himself! He doesn't *need* anyone to feed and pamper him. It's not like he's a dog or something. Dogs are good buggers! You can kick 'em half to death and they'll still obey you, still fall at your feet like you're a bloody god or something and still be grateful if you toss 'em a crust of bread. They know their place. I like that."

"But why, Dude? Rodn…"

"Listen, Mate, I've had it up to here with him. He does exactly as he pleases. He's a bloody nuisance and we can't have him setting off the alarms every night. Got it? The bloody owners come down on *my* head. There are insurance issues and *I'm* the manager here, Mate. *I'm* the one responsible!"

"But he keeps the rats and mice under control in the yard and keeps them out of the shop. We can't just chuck him out."

"Listen, Mate, we don't *need* him for that! A couple of traps, maybe some poison... Sorted! I don't *care* what you do with him; just do it, okay? Get rid of him. *Today*!"

"But he's been here *ten years*! And the customers love him; the animal lovers will go batsh..."

"Bugger the bleedin' bunny-huggers! Take him up to the dam or somewhere, and just turn him loose. If you're too chicken..."

"Sorry. No can do, Boss. Perhaps it's time I found myself another job."

"Yeah, Mate, I think it is. I'll just deal with the bloody problem *myself* this afternoon. You lot are all useless."

My former place of employment which was also my home.

The Journey Begins

The lonely hours of the night slowly bled away into a grey dawn, promising rain. I poked my nose out from under the clump of flax which had provided scant shelter from the biting wind. My sense of smell told me only one thing: everything was unfamiliar. Nothing else. I had absolutely no idea which of the strange new smells signalled danger, but I was much too cold to remain motionless any longer. I stood up, arched my stiff, aching back and cautiously emerged. Scanning the terrain around me, desperate for something familiar on which to pin my hopes, circulation slowly returned to my freezing limbs. Even my tail was cold. There was nothing I recognised, not a thing. I was all alone, far from home and I had no idea why.

Suddenly overcome by an overwhelming sense of panic; a terrible, terrible sense of anxiety and separation, I howled and howled at the top of my voice, running a few paces to the left and then back again, then to the right, this way and that I whirled around and around in distress, terrified of my own tail. I called for warm, safe hands to come and rescue me, to come and scoop me up. I wanted to feel the familiar, reassuring warmth of a human cuddle. I wanted to flop down on my pile of papers on the counter; I wanted to be home, in my shop, up on the shelves or out at the back watching them unload stock from the truck, but no one heard me, and no one came.

My agitation disturbed a blackbird in the nearby Koromiko bush. Shrieking in alarm, he made a hasty exit. This sudden noise startled me and brought me back to my senses. Reality broke through my consternation. I, Rodney, at the peak of my career, adored by so many friends, had suddenly and unexpectedly been dumped in the middle of nowhere, miles from anything vaguely familiar. I had lost my job, my purpose in life, my home, my family, my security and with them every shred of self-esteem.

I was utterly bewildered by the enormity of my situation and its implied consequences. How could this have happened? Why? How was I going to resolve my desperate situation? I tucked myself back under the thin screen of flax, sat down and decided to have a wash. Washing, I find, is the best way to calm one's mind and regain composure. First, I twisted my neck as far back as it would go and washed my back. I licked vigorously, trying to banish the taste of that vile man. The odour of his hands repulsed me, but I persisted and soon there was no trace of him there.

Next on the maintenance schedule were my back legs and hindquarters. I sank down onto a patch of soft, new grass and made myself comfortable, leaning against a large stone for support. One at a time, I extended each leg into the air past my ears and carefully cleaned every inch, paying particular attention to my toes. I cleaned my toe-beans until they shone. I nibbled at my claws, neatly trimming each one with my teeth. When I was done, I sat up and stretched my magnificent tail out behind me. Twisting with the flexible ease of my kind, I worked my way down the length of it, removing burs and fragments of grass as I went.

At last, satisfied that my hindquarters were in a state befitting the king of beasts, I began on my forequarters. Licking at a curled paw, I wiped it across my face several times. I repeated the paw-licking action, then wiped the back of my ears and the top of my head. I changed paws and duplicated the process for the other side of my face. Next, I carefully stuck my left front leg out and nibbled and licked at the fur. I spent a considerable time at my elbow where I had accumulated a sticky substance from the floor of the brute's car. It didn't taste too bad - most likely some residue from his last take-away meal - but there had been all manner of things on the floor of his vehicle. I gave my right front leg the same treatment and finally, with great pride and satisfaction, I began working on my bib. I drew my head back, tongue out as far as it could go, and leaned forward, drawing it all the way down the length of my chest in a long, slow motion. I did this several times, covering the whole area. I combed the ruffled fur meticulously with my teeth and tongue until my beautiful bib was once again its usual sparkling white.

I felt better after all this. I always feel good when I am clean. It's just the way cats are. I was able to think clearly now: somehow the act of washing unclutters the mind. I hopped onto the stone I'd been leaning on and sniffed at the air. A light breeze was coming from the West. I sniffed again, frowning with concentration. There was nothing on the air to give any indication of what I should be doing next.

I was hungry. My last meal had been yesterday morning, and I'd been used to dining lavishly before the shop closed for the night. Some might say I was a lazy, spoilt freeloader playing on human sympathies, but I *know* I earned my keep. I brought my fair share to the table. Admittedly, mice and rats were not much to my taste, nor were they apparently to the liking of my human colleagues, but no one could say I didn't contribute. In return for my services in vermin control, I was given two square meals a day. I was also used to getting pats and treats from adoring fans and friends. Many visited the shop only to see me, but they invariably left with a few small items. I was good for business and competent at my secondary role in Sales and Customer Service. Many customers chose to shop there because of me, and I always gave them what they had come for: a satisfied, rumbling purr from deep inside my throat whenever someone stroked my back or tickled my chin. They left with happy smiles. Oh, how good it had felt to have large, rough tradie hands smoothing my fur! I loved brightening their day, and I loved my job!

The simplest solution would be to head back to the shop immediately. Scientists believe that cats may be able to sense Earth's magnetic fields: the iron components in our skin and our inner ears may act as a natural compass, they think. I have no idea how it works, but my sense of direction was clear: it told me I had travelled from South to North last night, and so I started off in the opposite direction, homeward bound. But something hazy stirred in my mind. I hesitated. Why did my feet not wish to take me back in the direction I had come – to the only home I remembered? I frowned and sat down for a moment to think. It was no good. I couldn't make sense of it, so I set off again determinedly southward.

At first, I trotted down the road that had brought me to this place. There were no cars out and about, especially not this early, but the residual smells of tyre rubber and petrol fumes made me nervous. I veered away from the road and its unfamiliar smells and struck out into the bush with its unknown dangers.

I moved on for a while at a brisk pace, but then it began to rain. At first, it was only a soft drizzle which I tried to ignore. I didn't particularly like the feeling of water droplets on my whiskers, but I gritted my teeth and pressed on with purpose. Soon the rain was pelting down harder and harder. Cold, stinging drops penetrated my thick fur coat all the way to my skin. I was cold, wet, lonely and hungry. I sat down on the muddy earth, my beautifully-groomed coat now a freezing, sodden mess. I looked for shelter but there was absolutely nothing I could crawl under or into.

Utterly wretched, I sat crying miserably in the mud for a while. I sobbed and sobbed but nobody heard and nobody came. I could barely open my eyes. There was water everywhere, streaming down my face, pooling in my ears and all around me. Even the air I was breathing seemed saturated. I coughed and sneezed, then stood and shook myself, desperately trying to rid my coat of the unpleasant wetness. It didn't work.

Eventually I just lay in the mud, utterly dejected. I wanted to die, there and then. I'd have gladly traded one of my nine lives for the warm, cosy spot on the top shelf at the shop. I'd have traded another for a plate of Jimbo's Veal and one more to feel an adoring human tickling me under the chin and telling me what a handsome boy I was. Sadly, I have only one life despite the popular man-made myth, so I made up my mind: I wasn't prepared to forfeit it just yet. I still had the will to survive.

The First Farm

I was bone-tired by nightfall, footsore, cold and very hungry. The relentless rain had persisted all day as I trudged mile after wet, weary mile through sodden bush and pastureland. It was the smell of food that broke through my dampened spirits. At first it was almost imperceptible, but it expanded until it became the only thing I could sense.

In the cold, gloomy darkness of my second winter's night in the wilderness, a building loomed ahead. It was barely visible but for the welcoming glow of electric light spilling from its windows. Light meant humans! And humans, of course, meant food! I stopped and sniffed, savouring the aroma of cooking meat drifting on the saturated air. My belly rumbled in anticipation, and I swallowed hard.

I made my way cautiously down the slope through a thick tangle of wet grass. To the left of the human house was a small shed. I headed for the meagre shelter of its eaves and sat tiredly on the cold, hard earth to evaluate my options.

I shook myself vigorously, droplets flying from my once glossy coat in all directions. I felt marginally better out of the rain, but a wash was called for. As I licked myself, cleaning and combing my fur, a flicker of hope returned. My faith in humanity had been severely shaken, but I clung to the idea that humans still represented love, shelter and care.

When I had made myself as presentable as I could under the circumstances, it was time to make my appeal. I drew myself up on my toes, arched my aching back, then lowered my chest and stretched my stiffening limbs. I was Rodney, the most popular cat in Marton: these people would have to appreciate that, respect and pamper me as I deserved. I made my way confidently to the back doorstep, following the mouth-watering smell of their tea wafting from the kitchen window.

Sitting neatly with my tail curled around my paws, I politely asked them to open the door and let me in. Nobody answered. Perhaps they hadn't heard me. I tried again, this time a little louder. Still no reply. I had to make them hear me. I cried and cried, as loudly as I could but the door remained firmly shut. Starting to get desperate, I howled my plight, appealing to the occupants to take me in and feed me.

Suddenly the door flew open, and I was met with a bucket of cold water in the face! In utter shock and fear, I fled the way I had come. Never in my life had I been treated like this! The sheer horror that humans could be so callous and cruel!

.

When I was sure I hadn't been pursued, I slowed to a halt. I looked over my shoulder at the distant farmhouse. I didn't have the courage to try again, even though my belly was aching and spasming with hunger and I was again soaked to the bone. There was nothing for it but continue my quest for home. I walked wearily on, ever southwards, until I was too exhausted to continue. I was light-headed with hunger, but I also needed rest. Ideally, I was looking for a warm, dry place to recover but there was nowhere I could see. I curled myself up into a little ball, as tight as I could manage on sodden and muddy grass. I lay there in my misery, all hope lost. I no longer cared if I lived or died, so complete was my despair.

Don't give up after the first failure.

Feeling lonely and unwanted is the heaviest burden to carry.

Rainbow Bridge Tributes

Tiffani by Karen Chapman

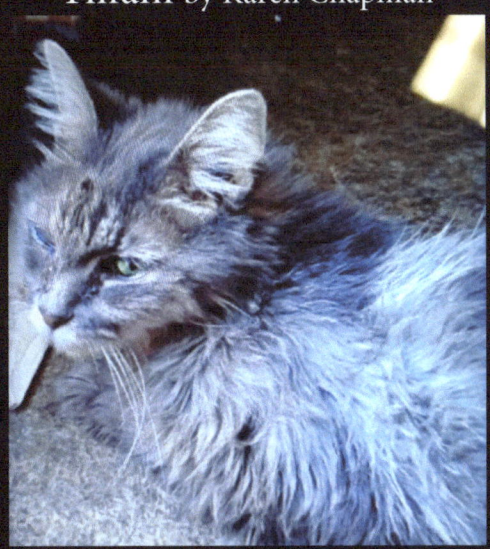

I've had numerous beloved pets over the Rainbow Bridge, but the one who held the most special place in my heart was Tifanni. She came into this world between the walls of our barn. When she was merely four weeks old, her mother abandoned her, leaving behind an 8 oz bundle of fur. Tifanni, a long-haired tiny creature, was small enough to fit in the palm of my hand.

From the start, it became apparent that Tiffers had some health issues. Her mother must have known this. I diligently attended to Tiffani's health throughout her nearly 18 years of life. She had a close bond with me, experiencing separation anxiety whenever I was away, except for work. She'd sleep by my side, and while I sat, she would curl up on my neck just beneath my ear, allowing me to hear her comforting purr. In her passing, I chose to have her cremated, with the intention of having her alongside me in my casket when my time comes, ensuring that we will be together for eternity.

Sam by Jill Brown

Last April, Sam passed away unexpectedly, shattering my heart. The rawness of grief continues to weigh heavily on me, and I find myself still grappling with his absence. A friend recently sent me a text that read, "Yesterday I looked at your photo and smiled, today I cried." The intensity of this pain is something I never anticipated.

Jerry by Judy W. Cady

I welcomed Jerry into my life when he was 11 years old, after he was given up by a woman on Long Island, NY due to her stroke, which made it difficult for her to care for him. I met her daughter halfway to take Jerry, and I maintained contact with the family afterward. Jerry was an incredible boy—affectionate, amiable, and even allowed my grandkids to pick him up. At the age of 18, Jerry passed away due to a stroke, coincidentally on the very day his original owner was laid to rest. It's a comforting thought that they are now reunited. Bless them both.

Rainbow Bridge Tributes

Mr. Whippy by Deb Brewer

Meet my cherished feline, Mr. Whippy, an Oriental Havana. Aware of his potential short lifespan due to a heart condition, the breeder, touched by his remarkable personality, offered him to me instead of considering euthanasia. Despite the initial uncertainty, we shared seven beautiful years together. His endearing nature effortlessly charmed even those who claimed to dislike cats. Affectionate and tender with his human companions, he exhibited a feisty spirit around other felines. Although he's no longer with us, the void he left behind is deeply felt and he is dearly missed.

Gizmo by Anne Tullock

Gizmo departed three weeks before his 16th birthday, just before Christmas. Every year, we'd take him for walks around the streets adorned with Christmas lights. People would often stop to pet him; he was a regular wearer of his Santa hat. He was an extraordinary cat, always eager to meet and greet everyone. I'm certain he's now sharing Rodney's role. His presence was well-known throughout the neighborhood. He'd perch at the end of the driveway, capturing the attention and affection of passersby. In his prime, he even had a moment in the spotlight, appearing on TV and in the local paper, though not for the most honorable reason—being labeled a street cat burglar, much to the embarrassment of his police officer "dad." The array of items he brought home was astonishing, with some even being returned to their owners. He had a particular fondness for workmen's socks. Gizmo was the love of our lives and his absence is still keenly felt.

Jinxie by Jana Ketchum

Jinxie resided in my home for three years, although his demeanor was often challenging. When he ran away just before I was set to move 1600 miles away, my friend Kris kindly took him in. Unfortunately, he passed away after living with Kris for six years. Even now, I still love him and deeply miss his presence.

In the deepest darkness,
your inner light shines
brightest.

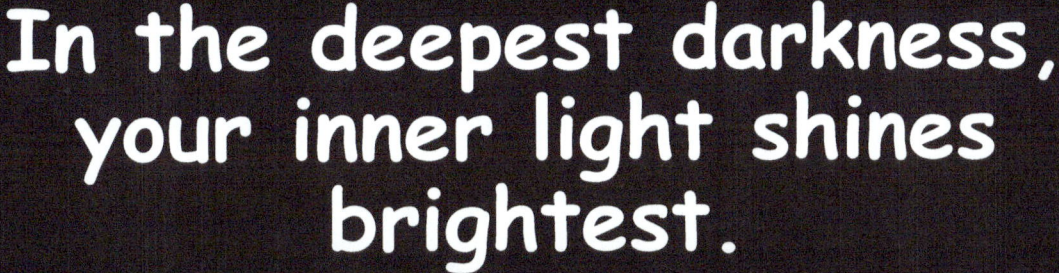

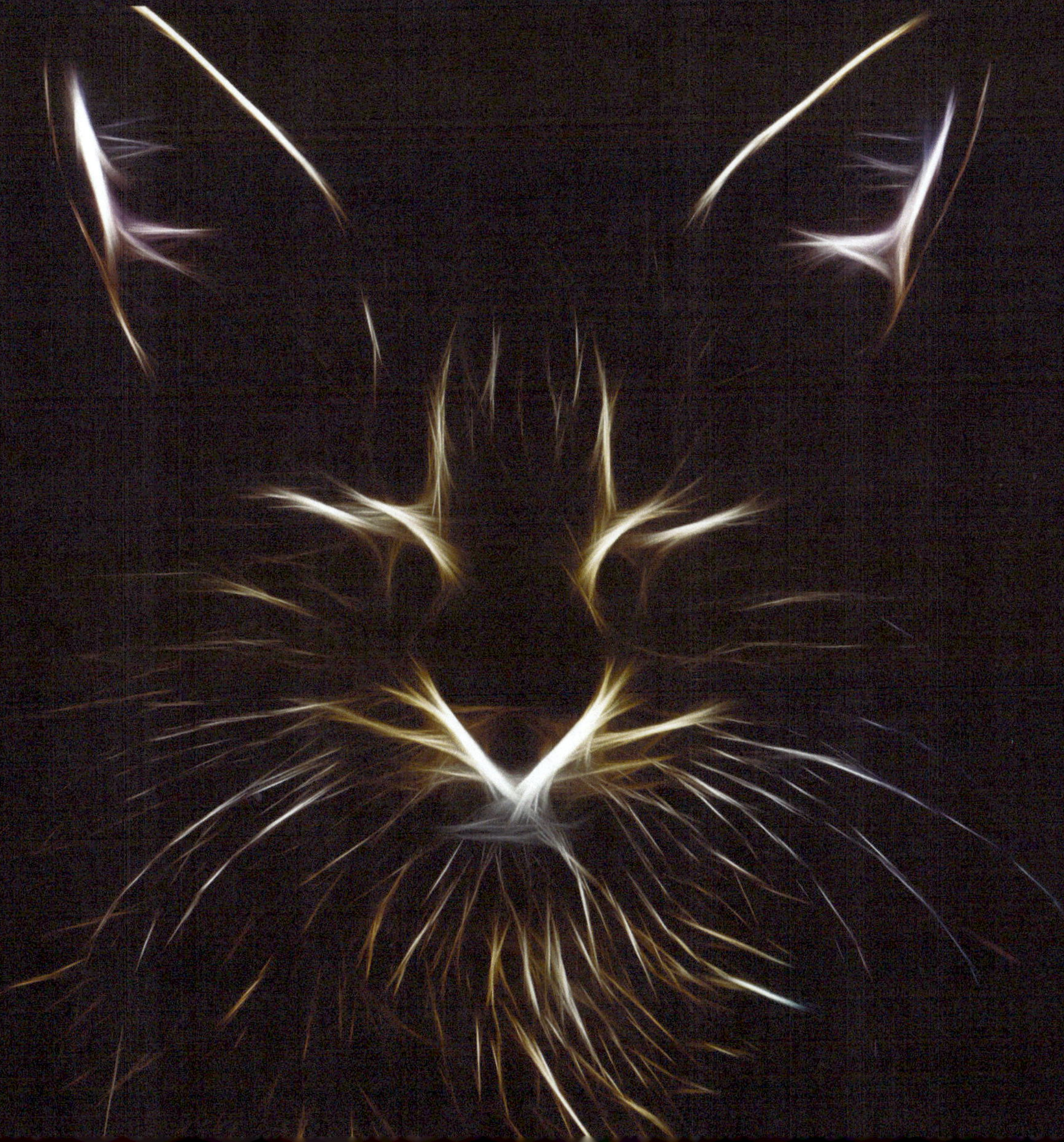

The Second Farm

Many hours later, the rain stopped but I was too disheartened to try and dry myself. By the time the sun came up and its feeble wintery rays reached me, I had fallen into a deep and exhausted sleep right there where I lay in the middle of a muddy field. When I became aware of my surroundings, the sun was already high in the sky. It was around mid-day and I was almost dry. I sat up, blinking in the brittle sunlight, dazed and groggy.

A short distance away, a curious creature stood eyeing me warily. I noticed another. And another. They were all around me, watching me, wondering about this odd little animal in their midst. They were big beasts, but I didn't perceive any danger. They weren't threatening me but were clearly puzzled by my presence. They were covered with dense coats of greyish-white fur which made them much bulkier than their skinny legs suggested. I stared back at them, fascinated.

I had never seen creatures such as these. I knew they weren't dogs – I had encountered those once or twice before and steered well clear of them.

They soon grew bored with me and lowered their heads to the damp grass. They pulled at it, grinding off tufts with their strange, flat teeth and chewing it in a weird side-to-side motion. This reminded me that I hadn't had a scrap to eat for two-and-a-half days, and my hunger flooded back with a sudden painful rush. I leaned forward and nibbled at a stalk of grass. These animals seemed none the worse for it, so how bad could it be?

But I was ravenous, so I gave it a try. I swallowed the first fibrous mass with difficulty, then another and another. I ate grass until my stomach stopped complaining, but all of a sudden and without warning it revolted. Up came the grass in a series of slimy spasms, but I did feel marginally better afterwards. 'How strange,' I thought. To this day, I still don't understand how sheep survive on such bland, tough and unpalatable food.

I was filthy and caked with mud, but I didn't fancy a bath after my grassy meal – the taste of stomach acid was still fresh in my mouth. Instead, I decided to familiarise myself with my surroundings before making up my mind about what to do next. In the bright light of day after a few hours of sleep, somehow my situation didn't seem nearly as dire as it had in the bleak depths of the previous night. I spotted a small copse in the distance and headed in that direction. From the lofty heights of one of those trees, I could survey the lie of the land and take stock.

I shimmied up the tallest one, as high as I dared go. From my swaying lookout, I could see hills rolling off into the North-West and felt strangely drawn in that direction, even though my instinct told me home was South. It took a while for me to work my way back down the smooth trunk: coming down is never as easy as climbing up, even for a cat! I slipped a few times and almost lost my grip completely, but eventually I was back on firm ground. I knew what I had to do. With renewed purpose, I moved off in the direction of Marton.

When the shadows were growing long, I spotted another human dwelling in the distance and decided to try my luck again. This time I would be more cautious. Little by little, I made my way to the farmhouse. I climbed into the safety of a small tree nearby to observe before I made my approach. The sun had slipped almost completely behind the western hills before I decided it was safe. There were no farm animals and there was no human activity. No sounds were coming from it nor was any light shining from the windows through the darkening twilight.

I sniffed around the back yard, investigating, all senses alert. The skeleton of an ancient ute lay rusting on its axles in a corner of the yard, looming through the shadows and long grass. I investigated all around it thoroughly. It was uninhabited, although my nose told me that it had been home to a family of mice not too long ago. I made mental note of the escape routes, should I decide to use it as shelter for the night. The back window was long gone, as was one of the side windows. The windshield was still intact, cracked like a spider's web, its glass yellowed and warped from decades of exposure to the harsh elements. I hopped up onto the back and peered inside. It seemed safe enough, so I eased my way in, stirring up a cloud of stale dust which made me sneeze. That was a good sign: at least I would have a dry place to sleep.

But I still had to find food. I jumped out of the side window and cautiously made my way over and around obstacles of logs, a discarded wheelbarrow and an old water trough as I approached the house. My senses and my survival instinct were beginning to sharpen after living the life of a pampered shop cat for so long. I could tell that the house was currently unoccupied. I walked around it, scanning for a way in. The back and front doors were tightly shut and couldn't be nudged open, even though I tried. All the windows seemed shut too, but then I spotted a narrow one high up – open just a crack. I had to try.

It was quite a jump to reach the high windowsill, and I barely made it in my weakened state. I scrabbled with my back paws against the wall, leaving muddy footprints on the flaking, white paint, but once there, I managed to stretch and pull myself up and over the edge and inside! Dropping down gingerly from the windowsill to avoid the open toilet bowl, I then explored the dark house, room by room, taking my time. My senses told me that people had been there recently, but not for a few days.

There was a small fridge in the staff kitchen back at the shop, and I knew this was where they kept my Jimbo's. Now I recognised the same thing in the kitchen of this farmhouse: it was indeed a fridge, but a much larger one. I sat in front of it and willed it to open.

two shattered on the hard wooden floor below, spilling their contents and adding to the mess. Hungry as I was, I didn't fancy the acrid smell of pickled onion nor that of chutney. I tried again, this time with a smaller jar. It broke into two pieces and its contents oozed out. The tantalising smell of Salmon & Shrimp Spread curled up from the jar and flooded my sense of smell. My mouth watered at the results of my handiwork. I knew people put this stuff on their sandwiches, and I'd shared many a delicious fish-paste sandwich with my colleagues back at the shop.

Nothing happened. I stood up against the door and clawed at its edge. Nope. It was no use.

Next, I nosed the pantry door open. It had been shut, but the hinge was old and loose and it was easy for me to nudge the door open with my nose and front paws. I leaped up onto the bottom shelf, sniffing at the cans and packages. I tore into an interesting-smelling paper bag with my claws. Flour spilled out in an avalanche. The white powder went up my nose, making me sneeze and sending little clouds into the air to settle over the nearby tins. I knocked them off the shelf one by one and jumped down to inspect them. None yielded up any contents.

Finally, I struck gold. I climbed my way to the top shelf which held all manner of glass jars and started knocking them over the edge. The first

I fell on my prize, licking ravenously at it until it was all but consumed. Determined to reach that last smear of delicious pulp, I stuck my tongue deep into the recess of the broken jar, but then a hot flash of pain exploded in my face and I jerked back reflexively. Another searing pain shot through my paw. The sharp edge of the broken jar had sliced through the delicate flesh of my lip and I had compounded matters by standing on a shard of glass.

Bleeding from mouth and paw, I limped away, wary of all the broken glass strewn across the floor.

Stinging pain overrode my not-quite-satiated hunger and I retreated to a bedroom where I lay down on the wide, empty bed. Blood slowly oozed from my mouth and spread a small, bright stain on the white counterpane. The damage to my foot was superficial and already scabbing over, but it stung nonetheless. As my body started to feel the benefit of my stolen meal, the pain subsided a little and I drifted off to sleep for a while.

When I woke, the congealed blood was clinging to the hair around my mouth and dry mud was flaking from my dirty fur. There was a metallic taste in my mouth which made me thirsty. I jumped down from the bed and went to the kitchen. Deviating around glass fragments at the pantry door, I sprang up to the sink and sniffed at the tap. I willed it to yield its bounty, which I could clearly smell. I knew water came from taps, but I didn't know how to work them. I batted it with my paw in frustration but water remained tantalisingly out of reach. I sat and thought for a while. There was no option but to make my way to where I had come in. There was definitely water there.

I balanced on the toilet seat, leaned down into the depths of the bowl and drank deeply. There's an old proverb that goes: Don't judge a cat unless you've walked a mile on his paws.

Back to the Dam

I stayed another day in that farmhouse. My mouth was sore but healing nicely. My paw hadn't troubled me at all after the first stab of pain and I was lucky the wound had been superficial. I'm a fast learner and I was now much more careful around that nasty stuff called glass. I'd also figured out it was only the small jars that could feed me. However, there were only two more of those, so I knocked them both off the shelf to smash on the floor below. One turned out to be Chicken & Ham and the other was my favourite, Salmon & Shrimp. Careful to avoid the shards of glass and sharp edges, I delicately licked at the paste, devouring the contents of first the one jar and then the other with relish.

I let myself out via the window and explored the weed-infested kitchen garden, looking for other sources of sustenance. Nothing smelled like food, and I couldn't detect the slightest trace of any

edible wildlife, not even a mouse. A fantail flitted about in a provocative little dance just out of reach but grew bored with the game and zoomed off. I re-examined the broken-down ute. The mice that had once lived there were long gone. Without a ready source of food, there was no reason for me to stay, much as I had liked the soft, cosy bed inside. I needed to get home.

As night fell, I allowed myself the luxury of a short catnap on that lovely bed. I left a nice collection of my hair on it for the people to find, and I'm sure this little gift more than made up for the food I'd eaten and the mess I'd made in their kitchen. I've found that humans are strange creatures who, for some reason, like to gather up our old, discarded hair although I have yet to figure out why they do this or what they do with these collections. Nevertheless, I was certain the inhabitants of that farmhouse would appreciate the gesture. There was nothing I could do about the bloodstains or the muddy pawprints, but I thought the composition looked rather pleasing. I have an eye for aesthetics and an artistic touch, even if it is inadvertent. Someday I might explore my talents further, but for now I need to continue telling my story.

Compelled to move on, I slept only lightly. Just before midnight, I found myself on the road again (in a manner of speaking) and hungry.

As I was passing out of the yard, a sudden twitching movement in the long grass caught my attention. I froze like a statue and watched. Although I hadn't been an enthusiastic hunter at the shop, my latent instincts were really kicking in now. Hunting meant survival. It was no longer a hobby or ploy to get humans to think they owed me board and lodging, and I realised I had been spoilt and entitled. Sure,

I'd kept pests under control, but had I really given it my best? Was I so good at my job that they couldn't get by without me? Evidently not.

I crept across the empty yard, keeping downwind of the tantalising movements, every muscle tensed, every sinew taut and... pounced, quick and sure. I missed. I had not had experience with this calibre of prey. These farm mice were a lot sharper than their lazy, fat town brethren who were even more complacent than I had been. I leapt too far, right over a pair of them who had been squabbling over

a discarded apple core and they fled in terror, too quick for me to chase. I was disappointed and confused. I was starting to seriously question my abilities, so I sat down for a quick wash.

I soon realised that self-doubt and insecurity weren't going to get me where I needed to be. The sensible thing to do would be to head home and prove to my employer that I was indeed competent and capable in the hope of being given my old job back.

Looking out across the open grassland to the South, something stubbornly still didn't feel right. I shook my head and tried to clear my sense of confusion and unease before resuming my moonlit quest, trotting half-heartedly in a southerly direction. No. I hadn't gone far before I sat down again to survey. I was very uncertain about the heading I should be taking. I knew I had come from the South, but it didn't feel right to go that way. I don't know why, but I felt compelled to head North-West. My internal dialogue pulled me back and forth for some time, and in the end I reasoned my best course of action was neither.

I decided to turn around and head back North to the spot where I had been abandoned and wait for someone to pick me up. I was sure this whole thing had been a misunderstanding. Right now, there could be someone waiting for me or on their way to collect me from where that horrible man had dumped me. They weren't all like him. I knew many humans who loved me and who had my back. And so, I found my feet carrying me back to the spot where I'd been ejected a few days earlier.

The familiar sight of human habitation loomed, and I skirted around it to the West in a wide arc. I was not going to risk another deluge of cold water from that particular house. When I was clear, I stopped for a short rest. I lay down on my belly, chin on my forepaws, comfortable, yet alert. I became aware of the familiar smell of mouse. They were obviously unaware of the danger in their immediate future and hadn't smelled me yet. Narrowing my eyes, I scanned the surroundings without moving so much as a whisker. They snuffled and squeaked, foraging and scurrying about in their erratic, mousey way, closer – ever closer – to where I lay in wait, motionless.

I was in need of a solid meal and determined not to make the same mistake. I remained as still as I could and allowed the foraging rodents to approach almost to my forepaws, then pounced.

This time my aim was true. I bit through the creature's spine with a satisfying crunch and felt it twitch and grow still in my jaws while its companions scurried away in mortal terror.

I chewed up the mouse in a few bites, avoiding the tender side of my mouth as I ate. I had never enjoyed eating mice and rats, but I found this meal immensely gratifying. It hadn't been a particularly plump mouse and I wanted more. Triumphant, I went in search of another, the predator in me fully awake. I followed my keen sense of smell and tracked one of the escapees through a field, under a fence and into the next field. It didn't take me long to find it hiding in a dense clump of grass. With whiskers stretched forward, probing and gauging distance in the dark, I calculated my moves and in a split second the ill-fated creature went the way of its friend. With my confidence boosted and my belly appeased, I cleaned up, paying particular attention to my whiskers, before striking out to the North again.

By sunrise, I was recognising landmarks: the clump of flax I'd huddled under in that first terrifying night, the Koromiko bush, the stand of pines off to the left and the body of water in the distance. My once-soft toe beans were ragged and sore from trekking cross-country on hard, stony ground and I really needed to rest. I had been thirsty for hours – not enough to sample the muddy puddles on the way – but I really needed a drink now. I headed for the large body of clean water.

As I scrambled down the bank past the pine trees, my nose twitched, and my heart leapt for joy. I could smell home! The wonderful, comforting odour of cut wood tickled my nostrils. It reminded me of the neat stacks of cut timber in the yard and filled me momentarily with indescribable joy.

Ahead was a huge woodpile, its jagged logs and branches lying crisscrossed in an untidy pile, fern fronds curling up through the chaotic array. But all too soon, reality returned when I realised this was not home, only a familiar fragrance. I had lazed

Survival is not optional.

away many happy hours in the sun on my wood stacks which smelt just like this. The pleasant perfume triggered all manner of memories and emotions, and I was overcome with an uncontrollable, visceral sense of longing and loss. This most certainly was not home. I sat and let out a long, sighing howl; then another, and another. I lifted my head and wailed my loneliness from the core of my being, my desolation echoing around the empty wasteland.

A bank of cloud oozed in from the East, washing away the feeble sunlight and adding to the bleakness in my soul. My whiskers told me it was going to rain again. I pulled myself together. There was nothing to be done except make the best of my situation. Feeling sorry for myself was not going to solve anything, so I began inspecting the woodpile in detail, evaluating it for shelter and checking escape routes should I need to leave in a hurry.

A pungent smell in several spots told me that a tomcat had inhabited this pile of wood at some point and had marked it as his territory. I had no way of telling how long it would be before he returned to claim his kingdom: it could be hours, days or weeks. Previous encounters with my own species had not been pleasant. As a gentle-natured cat, I avoid conflict. I'm not very social when it comes to other cats, always preferring the company of humans. But what could I do? I had to choose between shelter and the risk of confrontation which would no doubt be violent. The dilemma left me panting anxiously.

Feeling sorry for yourself is a waste of time and mental energy.

Some photos of where I lived for nearly a month.

Rainbow Bridge Tributes

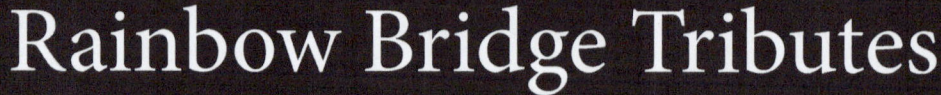

Romeow by Linda Deane

Dearest Romeo, you were the most endearing little ginger ball of fur, irresistible from the moment you caught my eye. Your loud cries echoed as you scaled the mesh of your enclosure at the shelter, insistent that I choose you too. Despite having already set my heart on Julie, you made it clear you were also coming home with us. And so you did, becoming a source of immense joy. Then, one day, seven years later, you simply vanished. Despite our exhaustive search, you disappeared without a trace. It's been nearly fifteen years since I last laid eyes on you, yet the ache in my heart remains whenever thoughts of you arise. I know you must be back in the safe haven of Planet Cat by now, and I hope your journey there was smooth, painless, and easy. Perhaps one day, the mystery of your disappearance will be solved. I've said farewell to scores of cats over the years but yours was the most excruciating because there never really was a goodbye.

Sophie by Susan Roberts

Sophie was my precious baby girl. We formed an unbreakable bond the night we welcomed her into our lives. It was an incredibly cold winter night, and to shield her from the chill, I nestled her inside my winter coat.

Which side of midnight she was born on is a mystery, so we decided to celebrate her birthday on Christmas Eve. We embarked on a 200-mile journey to bring her home from a friend of my brother. Sophie graced us with 18 beautiful years filled with love and delightful moments. She was my steadfast companion, especially during my struggles with migraines and other health issues.

Our mornings followed a cherished routine: sharing breakfast together. Before heading to work, I'd treat her to a tiny bit of cream cheese, and we'd tune in to the radio. Remarkably, Sophie had a favourite song – 'This Kiss' by Faith Hill. At the first few notes, she'd come bounding over to join me for breakfast. I even bought the single of 'This Kiss' just for her.

A few weeks after her adoption, during a family gathering amidst laughter and jovial conversation, tiny Sophie mischievously sneaked onto the couch and began tasting Dad's spaghetti sauce. As I jokingly scolded Dad for sharing with her, she brazenly started nibbling on his garlic bread too. Bringing Sophie along when I visited my grandma at the nursing home brought immense joy to my grandmother.

She was adored by the entire family but took exception to one of my sons when he moved out and bought a pet snake. Sophie fiercely hissed at him. In 2014, it was a heart-wrenching day when we had to bid farewell to Sophie helping her cross the Rainbow Bridge. We consider ourselves blessed for the 18 years of love, joy, fun, and unwavering companionship she shared with us.

Steinway by John Brian Cody

Steinway was the friendliest, most playful boy I've ever encountered. He got his name because he was always dressed formally, and his toes alternated between black and white, like piano keys - thus the formal name. He brought complete love and joy into my home, and I'm certain he's bringing it to Planet Cat now!

The Rabbits

Fat drops of rain suddenly began to fall and made up my mind for me. I crawled under the pile of logs to the driest spot I could find, deep inside. It rained for several hours, and I slept fitfully and uneasily. I was mindful of the tomcat and dreaded his return. Wind and cold I could deal with, but the constant danger of a cat fight kept my nerves on edge. I could even live with the dampness penetrating my fur in this temporary lair: at least I wasn't soaked.

While it rained on and off for the next few days, I did little more than sleep on the hard, bare floor of my uncomfortable refuge. Whenever it let up, I'd slip out to hunt and to check if my humans had returned. I sharpened my skills by snaring a Weta when it scurried out of a pile of rotten leaves. I had never considered eating insects before, but these were desperate times and I was ravenously hungry. I found that insects were an acceptable – although far from ideal – source of protein and became quite proficient at sniffing out bugs rendered immobile by the cold weather. I'm not ashamed to admit that I dined on many fellow inhabitants of that woodpile, cockroaches in the main. One does what one needs to do in order to survive. I also ate some larvae which tasted quite foul and never tried any of those again, no matter how hungry I became. They made me feel quite ill. The nearly comatose earthworm eased from a puddle of cold mud with my mouth wasn't as disgusting as it sounds but provided little more than a mouthful of gritty jelly. None of these food sources satisfied my hunger.

Every so often I would be lucky and find a sluggish skink or – if it was a good day – a mouse. I was still unsuccessful at catching birds this early in my adventure.

One morning, by sheer luck, I stumbled on a young rabbit while walking the track to the dam. It may have been her inexperience or that my hunting skills were sharpening out of necessity, but before she had sensed danger coming from behind, I had pounced and delivered the death bite to the back of her neck. This was my easiest, most substantial and delicious meal in more than a week. I polished off every morsel of the tender young rabbit, spitting out only tufts of fur and the bones which were too hard to chew.

Later that day, I couldn't believe my luck when I found a second rabbit lying at the edge of the dam, convulsing. I watched as it jerked and thrashed in spasms of agony until one last violent paroxysm relieved its torment and brought it the sweet release of death. I was still full from my earlier meal, otherwise I might have fallen on the fresh carcass with relish then and there. I reckoned I'd drag it back to my lair to keep and feast on later, so I sniffed at it while evaluating how best to get it there. It was a large buck rabbit, nearly my equal in size and weight. But something wasn't quite right. I could detect a palatable yet strangely artificial smell around his mouth and, as I tried to lift him by the nape of his neck, his head slumped forward and a few greenish-blue pellets fell out. I did not like the look of them. I inspected the odd-looking objects cautiously, sniffing at them and probing them with my whiskers. Somewhere in the recesses of my memory, alarm bells were starting to sound. I must have been quite young when it happened, very early in my career as a shop cat. I vaguely remember being told off by one of my colleagues: "No! Rodney, get away! That's poison! Don't touch it! Shoo!" accompanied by a loud clapping of his hands. Before I'd been given the job of Pest Control Manager, they'd used something quite similar to control vermin at the shop and in my first few days on the job, I had inadvertently stumbled on an overlooked cache of the stuff. As a well-fed, well looked-after, albeit rookie pest controller, I probably wouldn't have touched it, but the incident made a lasting impression.

I turned my back on the carcass and its dangerous pellets, and with a backward, scraping motion of my forelegs, attempted to cover the offending material as I would any object worthy only of the litterbox. I lost my appetite for rabbit flesh that day, and for the remainder of my stay at Hotel de Wood Pile, I did not encounter any more rabbits.

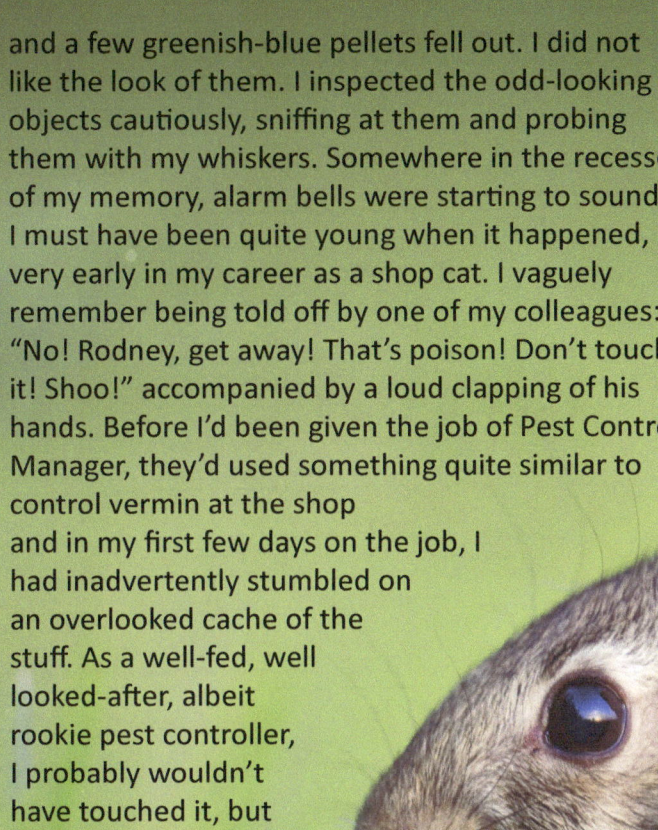

And so I waited day after dreary day at that dismal pile of wood for my old friends to come for me and fetch me home. Nobody did. As my hopes dried up and shrivelled away, my faith in humanity died too. I came to accept that I was friendless and alone. Never again would I share the warmth of human company; never again feel the caress of a soft touch smoothing down the fur on my back; never again would I curl up on a friend's jacket for a cat nap; never again sit on a warm lap to have my chin scratched.

The prospect of the hard, lonely life ahead filled me with despair. I had no choice but to fend for myself and survive on my own as best I could.

Meanwhile, back in Marton...

neighbourly.co.nz

Thursday, July 2, 2020

Cat dumping sparks outcry

MAXINE JACOBS

The SPCA has launched an investigation into the dumping of a beloved shop cat that had considered a lower North Island building supplies store its home.

Rodney the tabby had been a regular sight on the counter at Central ITM in Marton for almost a decade, lazing and sauntering about the shop.

But two weeks ago he was abruptly kicked out of town when the store manager took him to a spot 15 kilometres north of Marton and left him there.

Rodney's exile has sparked search parties near a reservoir where he was discarded, and remains missing. And there has been much discussion on social media about whether the animal has been dumped or "set free".

But a SPCA spokeswoman says there is no debate.

"Releasing" is returning a wild animal to its natural environment. Removing a companion animal from a familiar environment, and abandoning it, is dumping.

Central ITM Marton's branch manager has stepped down from the role and an inspector from the animal welfare charity is investigating the incident. Central ITM owner Robert James declined to comment, but in a reply to a Facebook post about

Main image, Rodney the tabby, a familiar sight on the counter of Central ITM Marton for almost 10 years. The business has apologised and is assisting with the search for Rodney.

Rodney, the store apologised for what had happened and advocated for the humane treatment of all animals.

"To the community, we hear you and we are doing everything in our power to make amends for the misstep taken. We would like to let the community know that the actions of one does not define the views of a whole company and ask that you acknowledge that our employees too have families and pets of their own to love, provide for and protect."

The store was working with cat rescue group Marton Moggies to search for and rehome Rodney, and was donating $1000 towards the agency.

A concerned ITM customer who alerted *Stuff* to the incident, said Rodney's ill-treatment was heartbreaking.

"In these times and all the advertisements about animal cruelty, SPCA, and not to dump animals, rehome if possible, how could such a thing be done?"

It's illegal to desert an animal in circumstances in which no provision is made to meet its physical, health and behavioural needs under the Animal Welfare Act 1999.

The SPCA spokeswoman said while some people may believe "liberating" their pet was in the animal's best interests, deserting an animal was likely to compromise its welfare and was unacceptable.

Marton Moggies has received reported sightings of Rodney near where he was dumped, but is yet to find him.

Traps have been set so the cat can be captured and rehomed, but some are fearing the worst.

Animals abandoned in unfamiliar environments are vulnerable to starvation, disease, injury and death.

ITM national marketing manager Juliana Raven said the matter had escalated more than necessary, impacting on the store, their staff and families.

* Mid-June 2020 - Rodney dumped 15km North of Marton.
* 23 June 2020 - Public alerted by a Facebook post by a member of the public.
* 24 June 2020 - Raye & Shane McDonnell begin searching in Marton daily and contact Rangitikei District Council for permit access to the dam as active pest management (i.e. poisoning) is going on there. Raye creates a Facebook page for Rodney. A rescue group becomes involved in the search.
* 26 June 2020 - Public apology from the hardware shop together with $1000 donation towards the rescue group's effort. The McDonnells organise flyers and distribute across Marton. The media is alerted.

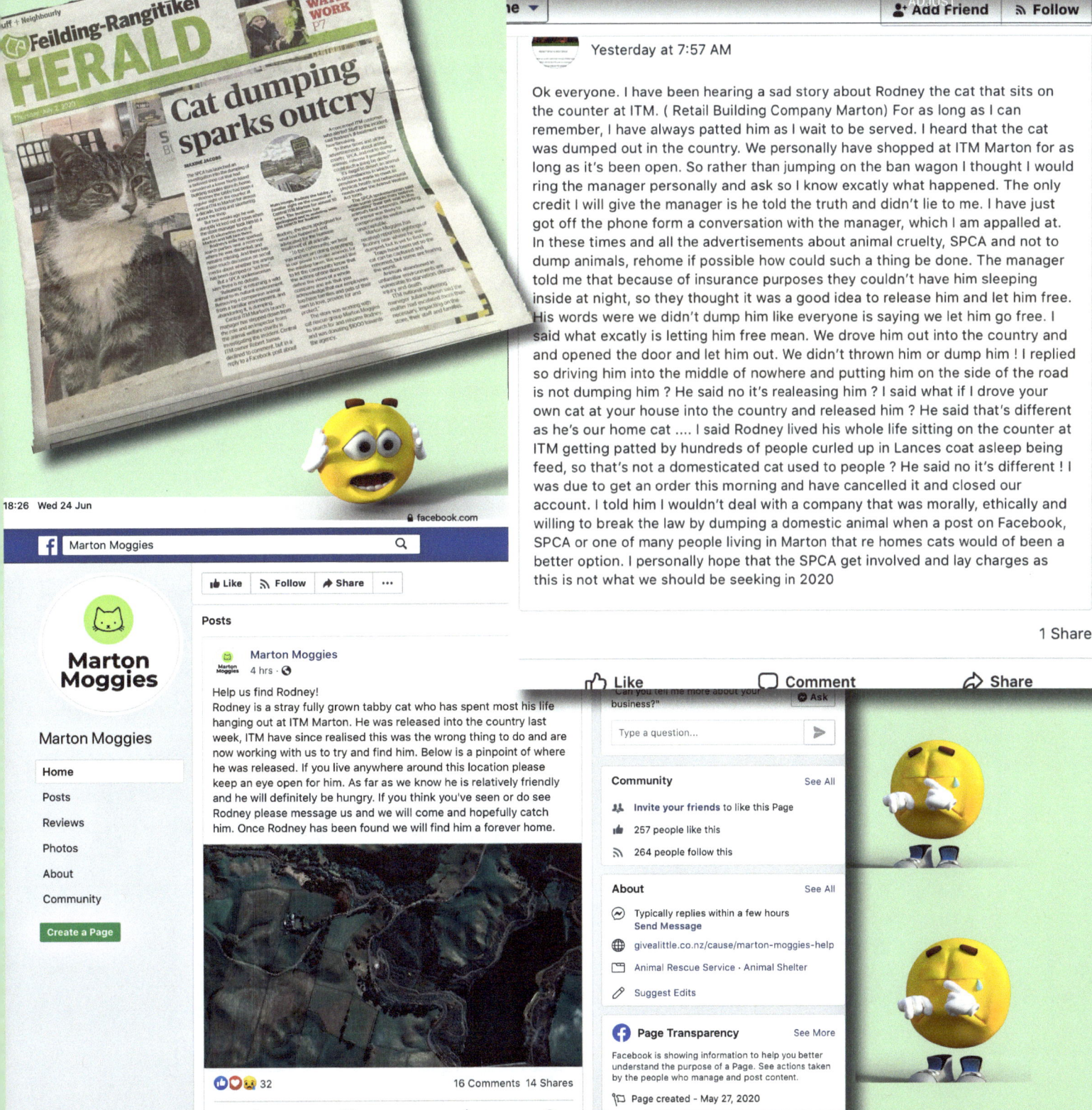

This is how I became: Rodney The Cat — World Famous In New Zealand.™

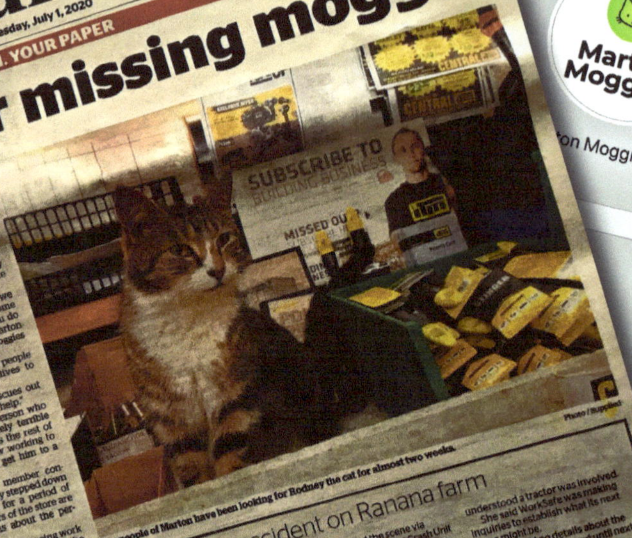

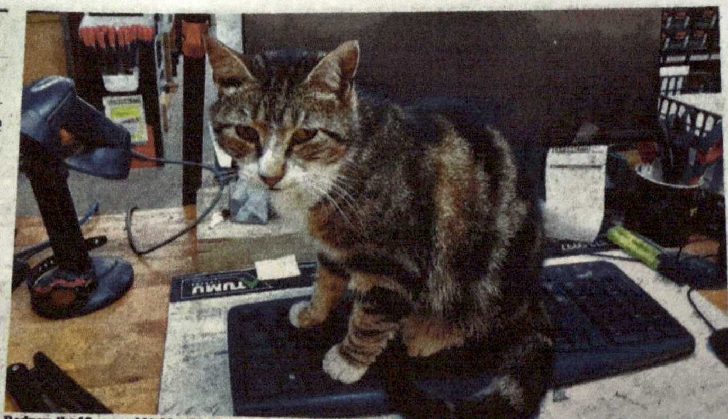

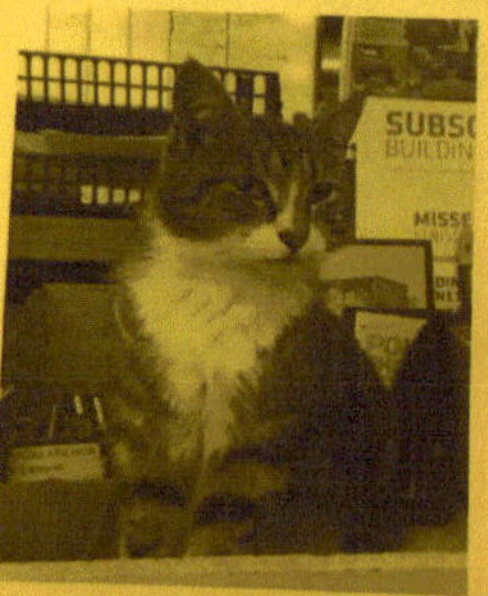

First Encounter

After two weeks of my miserable existence in the woodpile, having given up all hope of being reunited with the only family I knew, I started becoming aware of human activity in the general area. Strangers were coming and going, and they were clearly looking for something. Although I didn't know it at the time, these were friends – old and new – who were determined to find me because the news of my ordeal had broken in town.

Two weeks is a long time in a fifteen-to-twenty-year lifespan. It's certainly long enough to convince yourself that the world has cast you aside and forgotten about you, and I no longer felt wanted. I was afraid and my confidence was at an all-time low. People had let me down and broken my heart. I no longer trusted them.

One afternoon, strange metal-mesh boxes were left around my lair, and I could smell the most tantalising aromas wafting from them. I was tempted to investigate but hungry as I was, my fear was stronger, and I chose to watch and wait from the safety of my hideout. Not long after the people had withdrawn, a scrawny cat who looked a lot like me emerged from the bushes near the dam. He was pitifully thin. This was the cat whose den I had usurped! He was more afraid of me than I'd been of him, which is why he'd never returned and preferred instead to skulk in the shadows, evaluating me. I don't think he'd fancied his chances in an open battle.

I watched him jump on to one of the boxes and examine it suspiciously. He was hungrier than I,

A wise person once said, "Whoever you are looking for is looking for you too." Unfortunately I did not know this at the time.

and a little less cautious as a result. He got down and tiptoed inside, but as soon as he was in, with his mouth reaching for the food, a door fell shut behind him with a loud clang. I watched incredulously as the helpless creature thrashed about inside the trap, scraping his nose raw against the steel bars in an attempt to free himself. His screams of terror and anger echoed over the dam.

It fair chilled my blood. It proved I could not trust humans again, and I made the decision then and there to leave my woodpile in search of a safer hiding spot: one where I could not be found. I left the trapped Tom to his fate. I felt like a coward, slinking off into the bush after invading his home, driving him into the wilderness and consuming resources in his territory. I abandoned him as a sacrificial lamb and crept away from the only place of safety I had known in the recent past: it was no longer worth the risk.

As I was trotting off across a field of grass, I felt strangely compelled to turn around. I could feel someone looking at me: someone warm and compassionate, a human who radiated love and acceptance. I could sense *her* heart reaching for mine; *her* spirit calling out. I felt such a strong attraction to *her*, but I dared not risk the hurt and rejection of humans. My instincts told me to ignore it and keep going. If only I had followed my heart and not my misguided sense of self-preservation that day, my ordeal would have been over. But I was far from ready to trust again. *She* watched sadly as I ran off, putting as much distance between me and that place as I could.

Fear and discouragement

will tie you to the very place you do not wish to be.

Every storm will end. It won't rain forever.

Sometimes the storms you walk through are sent to clear your path.

Wild Wild Weather

I had unfortunately chosen the wrong time to travel out in the open. That night, the weather took a turn for the worse. It had rained throughout my stretch in the woodpile, but at least the sun had broken through once in a while and allowed me to bask in its feeble winter rays. Now I was about to experience the worst weather of the year.

It started with an icy wind from the South which tore at my ears and whiskers in biting gusts. It intensified throughout the night and by morning had become a relentless gale which was literally pushing me North. I trotted on and on, trying in vain to outrun it. Then rain began to fall in icy sheets. I couldn't bear the freezing drops in my eyes and the stinging pain in my nose if I faced South, so I presented my back and let it ruffle my fur from behind. Its icy fingers got under my coat, stabbing relentlessly at my chilled body. The storm raged on and on.

There was no prey about in this weather; no opportunity for me to recharge my dwindling strength. Even the insects had crawled deep into their burrows, beneath stones and inside crevices of bark and rock. I was the only being outside as Mother Nature raged and shrieked her fury. Low-hanging bushes provided scant shelter from the polar blast, and if I remained stationary for long, I grew unbearably cold. It was best to keep moving: I needed to keep my circulation going until I could find shelter.

The light was so poor I could barely tell night from day. After hours or even days of wearily forcing one exhausted foot in front of the other, I was in a state of trance. Subsumed by my misery, weak and tired, I lost concentration and took a tumble down a high, steep bank. I thrashed out with all four limbs as I fell, trying to grab at anything that might arrest my roll down the slippery gradient, but none of my efforts worked. I came to rest just short of the muddy, roiling waters below and was almost swept away by a raging stream. I could see it was rising rapidly.

I had nowhere to go but up. I was trapped by the rising floodwater and my only option was to claw my way up the vertical bank and onto safer ground. I lost my footing more than once, nearly falling back into the torrent. Finally, when I was close to reaching the top, I saw something: a hollow carved into the muddy bank by an unknown animal. I scrambled feebly towards it, barely conscious. My mind and body were starting to shut down.

It was a small, shallow space, not much bigger than I was. I found I could crawl into the hole and turn around to face outwards with some effort. A dank mat of rotting leaves on the floor stank of an animal I had not encountered before. The musky stench was overwhelming, but I was past caring. I didn't know if the animal was friend or foe; only grateful it wasn't home. I could borrow its tiny room to wait out the storm.

The downpour lasted a day and a half before blowing itself out. I spent all that time in my small, cramped space. When the weather finally let up enough for me to poke my head out and sniff the crisp air, my back and limbs were so stiff I could barely move. I crawled painfully out of the burrow – and immediately lost my footing. I tumbled back down the bank, thinking I'd surely drown this time, but the flow of the stream had subsided. I made a relatively soft landing on the muddy beach below and stood up warily.

I was not the only one who emerged at that moment. A small, teddy-bear-like head popped out of a hole near the top of the bank, a short distance from the one I had vacated. I noticed several hollows in the bank, but only two appeared to have been occupied: mine and this animal's.

Beady black eyes glared at me in fury, and then the creature came slithering and skidding down the bank towards me, baring its teeth in anger. Its long, sleek body was much smaller than mine, but this did not deter it in the least. The stoat was determined to punish me for taking advantage of one of its bedrooms and leaving without offering payment. She launched herself at me. I had nowhere to go but up the bank or into the stream – and I would have to get past her to reach the bank. In that split second, my choices were: (a) launch myself into the stream and risk drowning, or (b) dive past her and scramble back up the slippery bank on weakened legs and risk being torn apart from behind by an aggressive, determined stoat.

Standing my ground was never an option. I took to the air and sprang for the opposite bank, hoping against hope I would clear the stream, but I knew I was never going to make it. The icy waters closed over my head, and I found I was instinctively swimming. I kicked out and launched myself upward, coughing and spluttering as I surfaced. I paddled towards the far bank as the current carried me downstream and away from her. She hadn't given up, however. She was an excellent swimmer and was catching me up! As soon as my feet touched solid ground, I summoned my final reserve of strength and willed myself to run.

The stoat pursued me all the way to a large wattle tree and chased me up it. When I had reached the highest branch and could go no further, I turned and faced her, preparing to defend myself until death. I had the advantage of size and was positioned higher in the tree than she was. Now that she was no longer in her own territory, she weighed her options carefully, eventually deciding that the odds were not in her favour. I admit to screaming like a banshee with an aggression born of desperation, and with the sopping hair on my back standing straight up, I must have appeared more fearsome than I actually was.

She turned tail and scurried head-first down the trunk like a squirrel. I found that most impressive, especially when I had to make my own way down afterwards – I was forced to come down backwards, inching my way until I was close enough to the ground to jump clear. I've always found it more difficult to go down a tree than up it, and I think it's because of the way our claws work. Many cats find themselves stuck in this predicament and are scared to come down, but the secret is to do it backwards, slowly, without looking over your shoulder. Focus on unhooking one paw at a time and always maintain three points of contact. Don't ever think about attempting it head-first!

There was one good outcome of my encounter with the stoat: the unexpected dip had washed all the mud and grime from my coat, and with it the musky odour of stoat. All that remained was to lick myself dry, and at the same time to comb my fur into neat order with my tongue brush. As I've said before, I always feel better when properly groomed. Even though my once-glossy coat was beginning to look a bit tattered and my skin was getting loose from the involuntary weight-loss regime, I did the best I could to make myself presentable.

While washing, I contemplated what had just happened. It was my first – and hopefully last – encounter with a stoat. I subsequently learned that they are not native to New Zealand. They were introduced here, just as domestic cats were. They are more destructive than cats, but decidedly less than humans who are, I believe, the most invasive and destructive species worldwide. Stoats were brought to New Zealand by *Homo sapiens,* as were rats, mice, cats, dogs, rabbits, weasels, ferrets, hedgehogs, possums and many others that prey on defenceless native wildlife.

Homo sapiens is just a fancy name for human beings, and they have a lot to answer for. The first ones into this land brought dogs and rats with them, and together they absolutely decimated bird and animal populations, hunting many to the point of extinction.* Later settlers brought many other species: rabbits and hares, for example, simply for the "fun" of hunting them. But bunnies, like cats, are survivors and thrived here. Subsequently, humans in their "wisdom" brought in stoats, weasels and ferrets to control the rabbits which were now destroying pastures grazed on by their sheep, which had in turn also been imported.

All these mammalian predators introduced by humans wreaked havoc on New Zealand's native bird populations, especially those which made their nests in hollows of trees or banks, and those which were flightless. Examples: Kiwi, Mohua, Rifleman, Saddlebacks, Red-, Orange- and Yellow-Crowned Parakeets, and Kaka. Of course, humans had a further role in this carnage as a direct consequence of their logging and deforestation activities. They blame us animals for their own transgressions when all we are trying to do is survive in an environment they forced on us.

* The Penguin History of New Zealand by Michael King 2012 Edition

Kiwi

for the same resources. Stoats are agile, territorial killing machines with sharp senses – and teeth. They climb and swim. They are courageous, ruthless predators, unafraid of taking on prey or competitors many times their own size. Like me, they do what it takes in order to survive. They eat anything: rats, mice, rabbits, hares, possums, birds, eggs, hedgehogs, lizards, fish and even insects. They love Wetas! Yuck! That's where I draw the line. I won't sink my teeth into those ugly, crunchy bugs. No way!

You can draw your own conclusions about all of this, but stoats and weasels made it difficult for me to survive in the wild as an abandoned cat. I was competing with these ferocious, efficient hunters

Indirectly, stoats were the cause of another of my misadventures, although humans were ultimately responsible. I'll tell you about my encounter with the snare a little later.

Life won't get easier, but you will get **stronger**.

The search for me continues ...

* 26 June 2020 - Possible sighting of Rodney near woodpile at the dam.
* 29 June 2020 - The rescue organisation reports multiple feral cats caught in traps. One is very similar to, but not, Rodney.
* 5 July 2020 - Raye and Shane McDonnell arrange a roadside walk from the dam and back into town in search of Rodney with the aim of finding him, dead or alive.

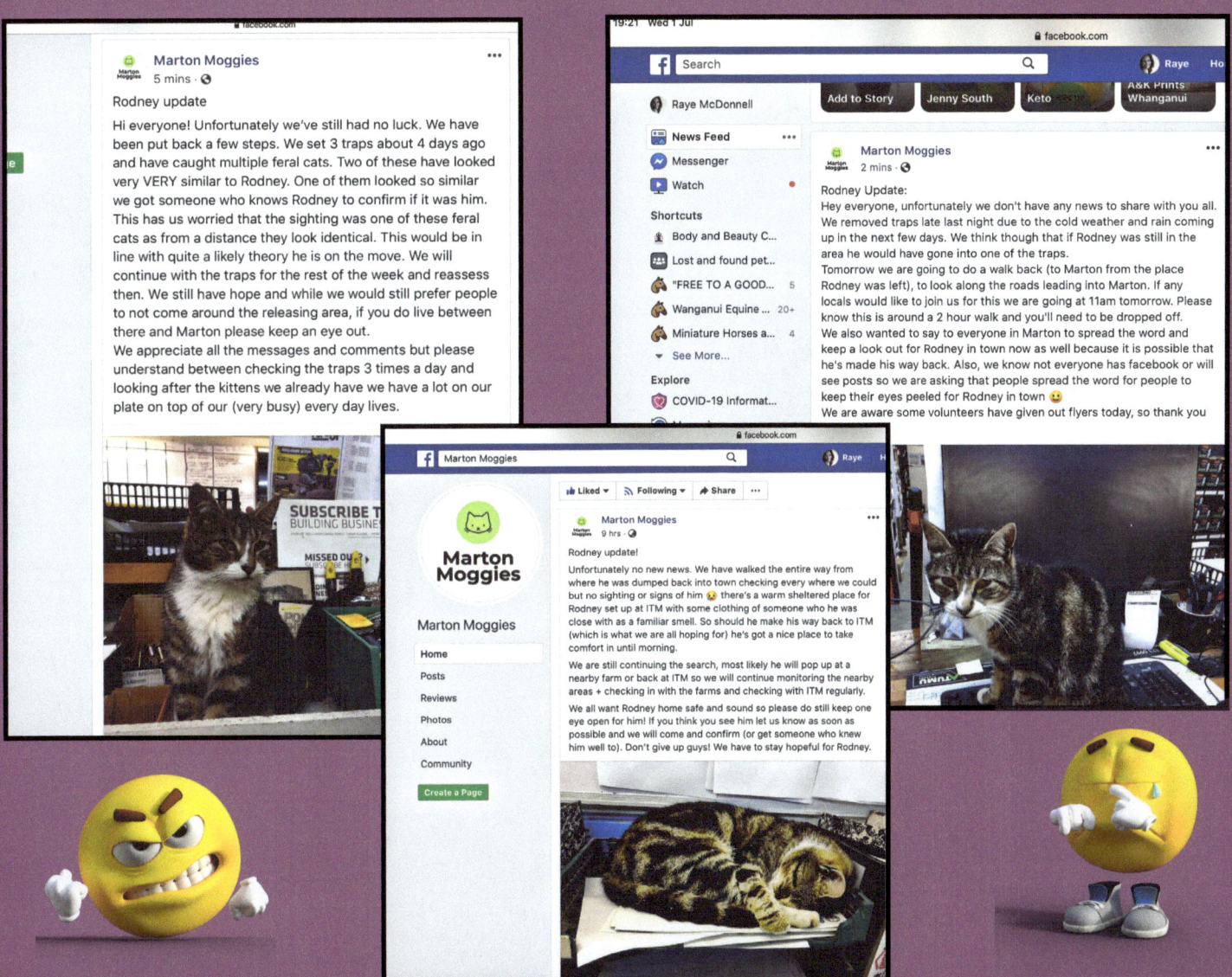

Skye by Terrie Ranson

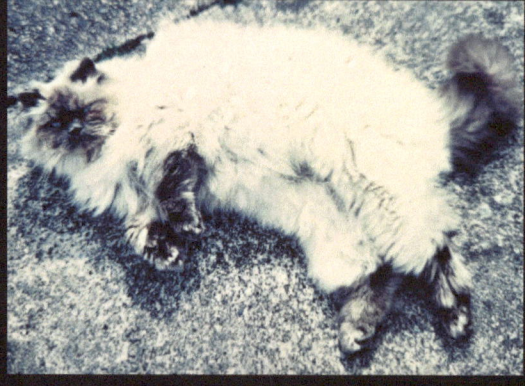

Skye, my beloved Persian cat was my first of this breed and had a remarkably dog-like quality, always by my side, whether I was in the bathroom, shower, or even the car.

One memorable day, as I was biking to work, he attempted to follow me. Upon hearing his meows, I promptly returned home, ensuring his safety by placing him in my bedroom. When I returned from work, I found he had playfully swiped and scattered everything from my drawers and bedside cabinet, almost as if to say, "If you confine me here, I'll make my mark!"

It's been more than two decades since my furbaby crossed the Rainbow Bridge, yet memories of Skye flood back, especially when I encounter other Persian cats. He truly was the most exceptional pet I've ever had.

Merlin by Adrienne Riggs

Merlin, who crossed the Rainbow Bridge 16 years ago, was an incredible guardian. During a tough phase in my pregnancy, one day I inadvertently dozed off after putting food on the stove to heat. It was Merlin who persistently roused me, eventually succeeding in waking me up. The food had begun to burn, causing smoke and flames. His determined efforts to wake me saved both my unborn son's and my life. Thanks to him, I managed to contain the fire before it escalated, and it all happened so quickly that I didn't even need to call the fire department. Merlin's swift response to the emergency was astounding. I continue to express my gratitude to Planet Cat and to God for sending Merlin into my life. He was a genuine hero, and I hold onto love and longing for him every single day. His protective nature extended even to my son, as he used to sleep in the crib, watching over him.

Rosie by Liz Treloar

Rosie loved resting peacefully in the warmth of the sun, in her beloved spot. She swiftly developed a heart condition and peacefully passed away with gentle assistance from the vet. We miss her terribly and won't ever forget her.

Sally & Leo by Jenny Woods

Upon our arrival in New Zealand in August 1997, we anticipated adopting a cat in the future. Little did we expect it to happen so soon. One day, my husband and our three-year-old son returned home from Porirua with a small bundle of black and white fur they discovered under a bush near the shops, now occupied by Pak 'n Save. That little ball of fur became Sally, a cat who knew her mind. She held the belief that she and I were a league above the mere males, be they human or feline, in the house. My sons often quipped, "Sally only loves mommy," a sentiment that held true - she merely tolerated them.

Every morning as I prepared my lunch, Sally would perch on a nearby step, eagerly anticipating her piece of ham. She possessed a distinctive longer eye-tooth, which we affectionately referred to as her "ham fang." Sally was unequivocally the princess of our household and made sure everyone understood it. She claimed a spot on my desk atop a piece of sheepskin, where she'd lounge and sleep. Sharing my oats porridge became a regular ritual for her, and much like Mittens of Wellington, she occasionally drank water out of my glass. Sally engaged in games of hide-and-seek, eagerly awaited my return home to accompany me into the garage, took every chance to rest in my car, called for my affection, and even 'assisted' in marking exam papers. She held a special place in my heart.

In late 2009, Sally was diagnosed with cancer, initially showing signs of recovery, but regrettably, it was short-lived. The final time I saw her was on Christmas Day in 2009. While we were on holiday in Auckland in January, Sally was under the care of my parents. On the morning of my birthday, her condition worsened. Despite our attempts, we couldn't secure a flight back to Wellington in time. My parents were by her side and provided comfort as the vet helped her transition to Planet Cat. We sat at Huruhi Bay on Waiheke Island, waiting for the vet's call, marking the moment she departed. The void she left behind in my heart was profound.

Leo, a mere six months old when I discovered him at Wellington SPCA, caught my attention with his resounding purr. He sported a peculiarly kinked tail, believed by the vet to be a birth defect. Leo was a not-so-brave lion. He was timid around people but held a deep affection for all of us. He'd exhibit great fear of my older son, but only when he ascended the stairs in his work shoes, causing Leo's hurried retreat, slipping on the smooth floor in his haste. The rest of the time he adored him.

Once, he disappeared amidst the agapanthus bushes, causing a frantic search and on a Guy Fawkes evening, his wandering caused me considerable distress. Fortunately, he returned before nightfall. Leo established a nightly routine of vocalizing his way down the passage, finally seeking solace on my bed where I would offer comforting pats.

Sadly, at a mere four years old in November 2017, Leo was diagnosed with cancer. Regrettably, we had to accompany him to the vet to peacefully transition to Planet Cat. He was an endearingly funny little fellow, but deep down, I knew our time with him would be brief.

Guns, Chickens and Dogs

I had given up on my quest to go South and was now following my strange compulsion to head Northwest. I couldn't explain why I was doing this – it was something far deeper than my in-built sense of direction, more like a mystical connection with someone or something. It seemed to be related to *her*, the one who was calling me back home day and night. Later, I heard it is a phenomenon known as "Psi Trailing"* which still baffles scientists despite their advancing knowledge in Quantum Physics.

Nature took pity on me for a while after that dreadful storm and blessed me with a period of pleasant, balmy days. Nights remained icy with brittle, frosty mornings, but I settled into an easy rhythm and started making good progress. The pads of my feet had become tough and leathery and I hardly felt the cold, stony ground any more. I found it safer to rest and recharge in warm, secluded spots during the day, so each morning I would fall into a deep sleep as soon as I was sure my chosen hiding place was safe, then wake when the evening chill returned.

I would arise refreshed but ravenous. My evening routine began with a good stretch followed by the important business of refuelling. Only after my hunger was satisfied would I continue my journey in earnest. Sometimes finding food took most of the night which cut into my travel time, but thankfully it was not the norm. It made more sense to keep warm during the cold overnight hours by staying in motion. My superior night vision made it easy for me to travel in the dark and gave me an advantage over my prey, many of which were cold-blooded and sluggish in the absence of the sun.

This sundown, I woke from my deep slumber confused. I had been dreaming of a warm place, an unfamiliar location filled with love and the haunting fragrance of a human whom I did not know holding me close and burying *her* face in my fur. As the dream faded, fleeting joy gave way to the dull sadness I had come to know so well. I had been fending for myself for nearly a month and was becoming good at it, but I couldn't shake a persistent sense of loss tainting my existence.

I yawned and stretched, then had a vigorous, satisfying shake. Fragments of the dry leaves I'd been sleeping on scattered in every direction. There was seldom enough time in my punishing schedule

* https://www.encyclopedia.com/science/encyclopedias-almanacs-transcripts-and-maps/psi-trailing

for the luxury of grooming: it was hunt/travel/sleep/repeat, but this evening I hesitated. Washing not only gives me time to think but is often a welcome distraction when I am unsure of things. It had been a while since my last proper grooming, so I decided to indulge myself. Again, I'd like to stress how important physical hygiene is for mind and body, and so I cleansed myself thoroughly while pondering my problems. I twisted my neck around almost 180 degrees to wash my back, licking vigorously at my unkempt fur. I singled out my paws for special treatment: they had faithfully brought me this far. When I was finished, I felt a new sense of purpose. There was nothing for it but get on with the business of survival. I couldn't let myself be distracted by a phantom from my dreams.

The mid-July sun was low on the horizon when I emerged from under the Kawakawa tree. I surveyed my surroundings: a large paddock lay before me, ending at the foot of a steep hill in the distance. I had been exhausted on my arrival at dawn and hadn't paid much attention to anything apart from the immediate safety of the tree. There was a smell of dogs about, but it was distant. Despite my therapeutic wash, I started thinking about my compulsion again. There had never been any physical signals for this overwhelming urge to travel in the direction I was going. I couldn't understand it then, but I do now: my soul was crying out for *her* love and the home *she* would provide. I was being drawn to *her*. As a cat, I didn't have to prove I could survive in the wilderness, but an even more powerful force was shadowing me, leading me home. Home to a place where I belonged.

The wind whispered in the long grass as I sniffed around my temporary lair. The smell of mouse was all about but there was no tangible evidence of them. These country mice were far wilier than their urban counterparts and at the slightest hint of a predator, they made themselves scarce. Out here, they had many more hostile animals to contend with and lived on a hair-trigger.

With the images of *her* starting to fade, I stopped dawdling and started moving away. Soon I spotted a farmhouse tucked inside the shelter of a huge hedge, halfway up the hill. I knew that human dwellings meant food. They also meant danger, but if I was careful not to draw attention to myself, I might be rewarded with an easy meal scrounged from discarded rubbish, or by preying on creatures who were similarly drawn to it.

I struck off in search of food closer to the farm and started detecting the smell of bird. I had now developed some skill in catching them, sometimes managing to swipe a lazy blackbird or slow-moving sparrow out of the air. I liked the taste of them, but catching creatures with the advantage of flight is always difficult. These ones were different. They smelled somehow… more bird-ish, and their tantalising odour drew me toward a squat building at the back of the main house. As I got closer, I could detect the competing odours of people and dog.

I jumped up onto the low wall of the building and peered through the mesh-covered opening above my head. A sea of birds lay settled inside, dozing companionably in the waning light. They were much larger than blackbirds and my mouth watered.

Clean on the outside equals **Sane on the inside**

I saw that they would be tricky to catch because of their size, but a single one would provide a substantial meal. I examined the mesh, stretching up and probing it with my nose. How was I going to get inside? I prowled the perimeter of the chicken coop, looking for a way to break in. On my second pass, I spotted it: a small gap where the nails were rusty and the mesh had lifted slightly from the wooden frame. I swarmed up the mesh for the gap located just below the tin roof, squirmed through it with the practised ease of a cat burglar, landed quietly on all fours and selected my target.

The chicken was easy prey and died instantly, but the unexpected disturbance triggered panic in the flock. A cacophony of alarmed squawking broke out in the henhouse which I had not been expecting. Instinct told me to abandon my kill and get out fast, but I was disorientated by the stupid birds fluttering and trampling each other in their panic and lost my bearings. I began to panic too which riled them up even further. It was bedlam.

In the midst this chaos came the angry barking of dogs and the shout of a man. They were approaching fast. I shimmied up the mesh and

scrabbled at the fasteners desperately, still unable to locate the gap I had used to get in. The mesh came away from the beam as rusty nails tore loose. Wounding my paws on sharp wire strands, I wriggled through the opening and flung myself out. I landed on my feet with a jarring thud which was accompanied by a stab of pain from my right shoulder and bolted away into the darkness just in the nick of time.

"Damned feral cat! Go boys, GO! Geddit! Find the bugger! Fetch, fetch, fetch!"

The dogs didn't need much urging for this was what they were bred to do. They raced after me yipping in high-pitched excitement while I fled for my life. The farmer swept his torch over the carnage in the chicken coop. Several birds lay dead and trampled. He swore under his breath, cursing me and all of my kind, but there was nothing he could do for them now. He set off in pursuit behind his dogs who were at that moment three-quarters the way across the paddock, but I was much further than that! The dogs gradually slowed to a halt and sniffed around in disappointment before he called them back.

It had been a very lucky escape. If I had reacted a second slower or if I had been unable to fashion a new exit, they would have had me. The dogs lost my scent when I plunged through the icy brook at the end of the paddock, and my swift legs carried me into the dense undergrowth on the far bank and safely up the tallest tree where I now sat, sopping wet, all my careful grooming for naught. My pursuers eventually gave up their search and I breathed a sigh of relief. I was angry at myself for having been so careless and complacent.

I settled as comfortably as I could in the broad branches and started grooming from scratch. There wasn't anything else I could do while I waited for the hue and cry to die down. In my estimation, it would be sheer madness to come down now – back in their yard, the dogs remained on high alert and would be looking for any sign of me. No: I was safe up here, and so I waited out the night on my lofty, swaying perch.

Conversations about me

"Hey, Bro! How's the week been for youse?"

"Yeah, nah, not too bad, and over at your place?"

"All right, much better weather these past few days, ay? Listen, Bro, I don't have much time: got to get the old tractor going an' all this morning, ay. I just wanted ta let youse know there's another bloody feral cat about. Lost a few chickens last night, ay. Would have shot the bugger if I'd had the AR handy, but he was too quick for me an' the dogs."

"Chur, Bro. Sorry about your chickens, mate, but thanks for the heads-up. I'll tell the missus to keep an eye out too. You have a good day. Bye."

"No worries, Bro. You keep well, ay. Bye."

• • • • • • • • • • • • •

"Hello. Is that the cat place, the rescue place?"

"Yes, how can we help?"

"I believe you're in charge of the search for Rodney, the missing Marton shop cat?"

"Er... yes. Have you spotted him?"

"I don't know, but our neighbour keeps chickens, and he alerted my husband about a feral cat on his farm. It got into his henhouse last night, but luckily it got away before he could shoot it. He hates cats and whenever one wanders up our way, he dispatches it pretty damn quick. I spotted a kitty in our barn this morning: white bib and grey stripes. I just thought it might be Rodney and I want him to be safe."

"Thanks for the info! Whereabouts are you? We'll load up the traps and come out now."

Found!

RODNEY UPDATE:

We have amazing news, we've found Rodney and he is now safe and sound in our care!

Earlier in the week we received a phone call from ITM informing us of a local who believed he was residing on their farm, they'd seen Rodney in the local newspaper and recognised him! We immediately set traps and within 3 hours we were picking him up. Rodney had trekked around 13km in the other direction (away from Marton) from where he was left! He has had a couple of days to settle down and we think his snuggles and purrs tell us he's happy to be back to the inside life 😊

We went to the vet today (the amazing Southern Rangitikei Veterinary Services Ltd) and he has had a full check over and has been microchipped and treated for worms and fleas. We want to say thank you to Central ITM for completely covering his vet bill.

In case anyone is wondering, we did confirm it was him with someone who knows him, just so we were 100% sure.

We are so grateful for all the support you have all given throughout the last month. We would not have been able to do this without the community backing us and the hours everyone in the area has put in to finding the wee man. We are beyond happy to bring you this awesome news! As you can imagine this has been a pretty intense journey for everyone and we are so stoked there has been a happy ending for Rodney ❤️

Rodney will be staying in our care for at least another 2 weeks while he settles down and we await some blood test results from the vet. We will make a post at a later date to find his perfect home.

On another note, we are very grateful for the support we've received in regards to the other kittens we've been rescuing (5 this week!). If you'd like to donate, our givealittle is https://givealittle.co.nz/cause/marton-moggies-help
😊❤️

Sunday 4:24 PM

I understand you'd want to see him however as mentioned we are just waiting and we are going off professional advice and not introducing him for to new people at least 12-14 days until he has settled down.

Totally understand that & more than happy to wait until Rodney is ready. As you can appreciate it has been a difficult few weeks for me personally doing everything humanly possible to help locate him so finally meeting him will help with closure. His page is still being bombarded by his followers. Are you able to send an updated pic or video and an update from your end to share to everyone in the meantime?

Yes definitely understandable it has been a hectic month for everyone! We've chucked a video on our page so please feel free to share it on there. We will also be doing updates so anything we post definitely share onto your page so people can see

* 14 July 2020 - Rodney found after being spotted on a farm, 14km north of where he had been dumped.
* 17 July 2020 - Announcement made.
* 19 July 2020 - Raye is eager to meet Rodney but has to wait. Eventually they do meet and Raye expresses interest in adopting Rodney. However, it is decided that Rodney should live with the family who raised him as a kitten.

... and that is how I found myself back in Marton, living in a new household. But before I ended up there, I met *her* briefly: the kind woman I had dreamt of. My angel. Suddenly it all made sense and I believed my troubles were over. I thought I would be with *her* forever, but still I was not the master of my own fate. *She* didn't have any influence in the matter either.

As a result of politics between others who had involved themselves in my rescue all chances of a happy-ever-after for me right there and then were blown. Despite *her* tireless searching and the effort she had expended, it was decided that I should live elsewhere.

Please don't get me wrong: my new family were lovely, but I knew I was meant to be with her. I didn't fit into that busy household. I've always been shy and introverted around animals and it was difficult for me to make friends with the other boisterous pets in the house. Although it had been different with humans and I had once enjoyed the company of lots of people, my experience in the wilderness had changed me. I had been emotionally scarred.

I didn't stay long. My new home was close to the shop, and I went back for the security of it. I knew some of the people there were no longer my friends, but I preferred the familiarity of my old address with its nooks and crannies into which I could crawl when I needed peace and quiet, away from the boundless energy of those dogs. The people at the shop kept taking me back. No sooner had I arrived, and I would be whisked back to the disconcertingly vibrant family whereupon I would start plotting my next escape. After several breakouts, my new people realised I was unhappy and found a home for me next door to the shop, but I am a creature of habit and carried on with my mission to return to my origin. I was overwhelmed by all the changes in my life. I simply needed the security of familiarity until I could finally be with *her*.

Management at the shop refused to cut me any slack and rang the SPCA without consulting either of my new families. The SPCA advised them to leave me at the vets where they would come for me and rehome me in a faraway town under a new identity. With heavy hearts, my new families acquiesced, and I found myself once again changing hands like a commodity to be either discarded or repurposed when it had expended its usefulness. Is it any wonder I lost my faith in humanity?

I hated that cage! I spent nearly two weeks in it. I was now known as Robby. My age had been altered to make me more appealing for adoption and my past had been concealed. The SPCA lady was nice, though. She kissed the top of my head and welcomed me with an apology while putting me into my new prison. She made sure I had a blanket, a litter tray, bowls of water and food – it was the best she could do under the circumstances.

After a comfortable existence in the shop, my adventures in the wilderness and the turmoil of not knowing where I belonged, I had a tough time adapting to life in a cage. There were so many scary sounds and smells to cope with and I felt claustrophobic. I couldn't see what was going on around me and the stress started taking its toll. My nerves were constantly on edge. I couldn't sleep. I had no idea what was going to happen from minute to minute and was forced into a state of permanent "fight or flight". There were dogs barking and howling, other cats constantly crying, shrieking children, men with booming voices and chattering women coming and going. Very few people had any regard for the mental state of incarcerated animals. The ebb and flow of frightening noise was ceaseless. Animals arrived and left. I had no idea if I'd be next and what would happen to me when I was taken. I was no cute, cuddly kitten or puppy. These, I noticed, never stayed for long. There was scant demand for older, somewhat antisocial cats like me. Humans are fickle, placing little value on the life of an animal who isn't cute, useful or particularly beautiful, and I'm a very ordinary cat.

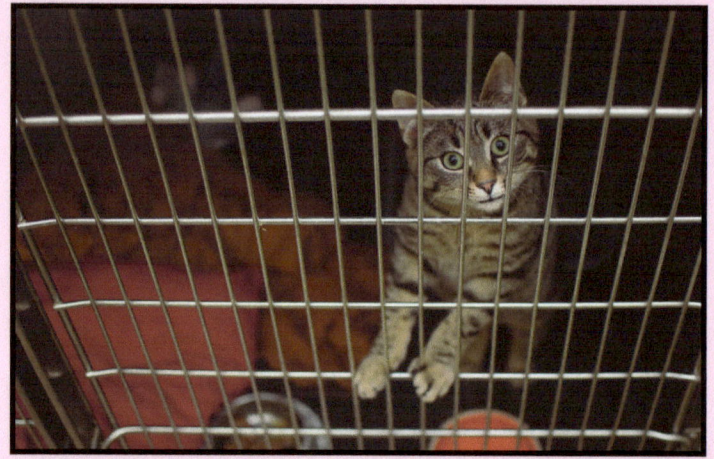

After a week, I was desperately unhappy and growing restless and irritable. I paced up and down my small space, howling and upsetting the other cats. It also tended to set off the dogs, some of whom howled along while others barked. It was around this time that I almost got away. The cleaner who came to hose down the cage floors forgot his wellies and nipped back to the storeroom to fetch them.

In his haste, he didn't secure the door of my cage properly and I took the gap. I butted at the gate with my head until it gave way and was out like a bolt of lightning! I wasn't aware of the additional perimeter around the cat enclosure until I came up against it, otherwise I would most certainly have escaped. When he returned and saw what had happened, I was ignominiously backed into a corner, recaptured, and returned to my cage to continue my prison sentence.

Shortly after my failed break-out, a young couple from Spotswood, New Plymouth came to adopt me. When the paperwork was done, they put me into a carrier and loaded me into their car. I truly hate car rides: every time I am put into one, I have flashbacks to that awful day I was so cruelly torn from the comfortable, productive life I had led. I'd given ten years of faithful service before being callously dumped in the wilderness in mid-winter to fend for myself, but it taught me to survive on my own. I had faced many dangers in that brutal month, followed by another three months of turmoil and insecurity in which I knew I didn't belong where I had been compelled to live. I was more unsettled than ever on that fateful day in October 2020 as the car pulled into the couple's driveway on Marama Crescent.

As they were lifting my carrier out of the car, a neighbouring dog set up a frightful racket and scared me half out of my wits. I don't know how I did it, but with strength and desperation born of terror, I freed myself from that box and ran. I ran blindly, desperately trying to escape danger.

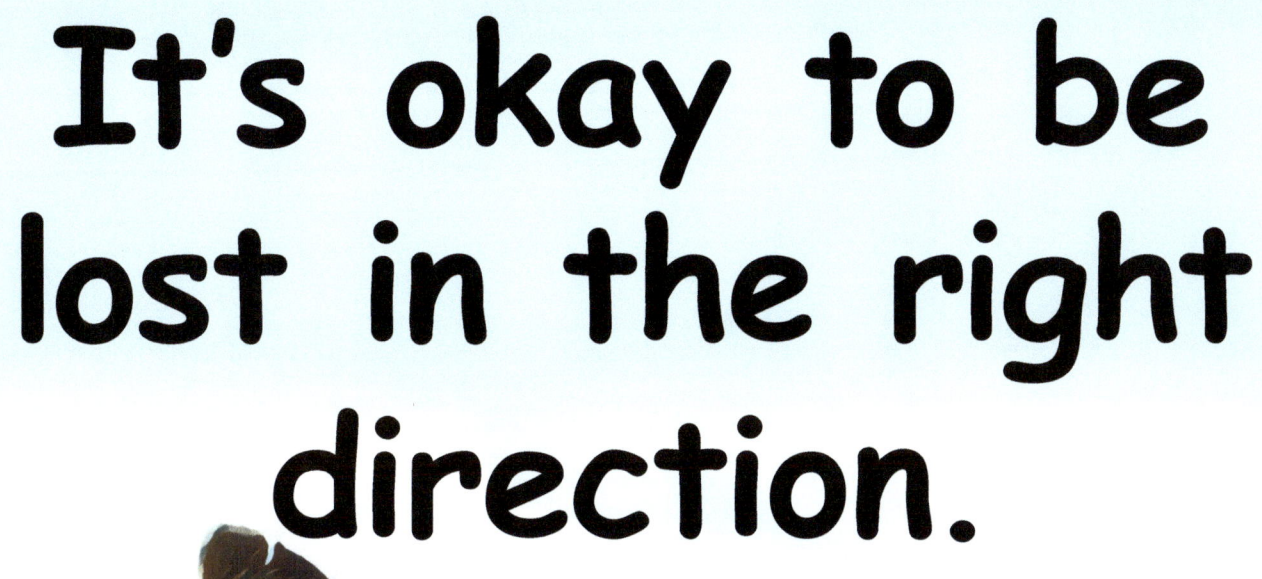
It's okay to be lost in the right direction.

Honey by Helen Povey

My daughter Victoria and I took our lovely grey cat Lucy to the vet one day. While there, we discovered that the vet was caring for a bunch of kittens that needed homes from the Upper Hutt SPCA. As we waited, we asked if we could spend some time with the kittens, and fortunately, the answer was yes. We eagerly opened the cage and each chose a kitten to cuddle. Then as I reached for another kitten, a playful and uniquely colored little kitten boldly nudged her way to me, settled in my hand, and immediately began purring. As I lifted her toward me, an undeniable feeling struck me—my heart and instincts confirmed, 'She's meant to be mine.' My wonderful Honey became a part of my life for almost 14 years. When she fell seriously ill and it was time to bid her farewell, the bond between us was profound. If I had been a witch, she would undoubtedly have been my familiar. Honey was a combination of sassiness, bossiness, and immense affection all wrapped in one. She held the title of 'The Queen of the Universe' in my home because she genuinely believed she had the right to be everywhere and on everything. Whenever guests visited, she'd nonchalantly saunter past, assess them, and determine if they were worthy of a pat, occasionally attempting to sneak into their handbags just to investigate if she could fit. Although I now have two other beautiful cats, the void left by Honey's absence is deeply felt. Her unique personality and unwavering presence are dearly missed.

Boo, Furby and Tigger by Bernie Mellon

My beloved Boo was absolutely purrfect. His passing in March 2022 left us all deeply saddened, and to this day, we fondly reminisce about him. Boo holds a special place in my heart as he was my very first rescued feral kitten, discovered around Halloween in 2005. He was a constant presence, always by my side when I returned home from work.

Furby, a kitten born to a neighbour's barn cat in 2001, was incredibly soft and affectionate. His departure to Planet Cat was in 2014, leaving a void in our lives.

Tigger had a more tumultuous entry into our lives — a neighbour witnessed him being thrown out of a car on the Highway as a 2-year-old in 2004. Despite his unfortunate start, he patiently waited in our yard until we returned from vacation and swiftly made himself at home. Though originally named Jake by his previous owners, (he had a tattoo but his previous owners couldn't be traced) I changed his registered name to Tigger. His love for Cat Grass was evident, bringing him immense joy. He departed to Planet Cat in 2017.

These feline companions, each with their unique tales and personalities, have left an indelible mark on our lives, and their memories remain cherished and ever-present.

Willow by Kate Moffat

Willow, my constant companion for almost 18 years, came into my life after being abandoned. She became my shadow, accompanying me everywhere, even to the most unexpected places like the toilet.

Sooty by Jacky Steele

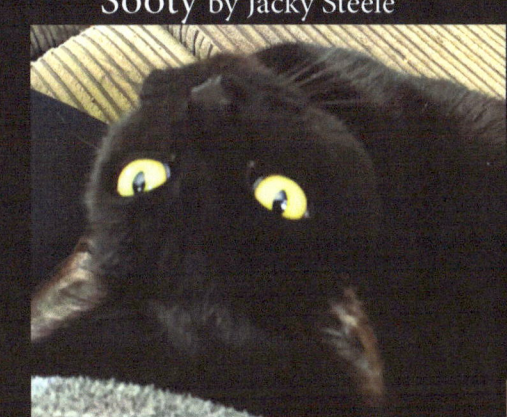

Sooty was the best, but daftest cat I've ever known. He taught me what precious souls cats are, and that they are the best friends a human can have. I sadly lost him in December 2022 he had a stroke at just 9 and a half years old. But he'll live on in my heart forever and a day.

Emmy by Carole Krammer

I trust Rodney has welcomed my beautiful and cherished girl, Emmy (7 April 2008 - 26 September 2023) at the Rainbow Bridge. Until we meet again, please take care of her.

TC, Nureyev, Barishnikiov, Tammy, Bubbles, Fiona, Emma, and Greta by Yolande Smith

I wish to honour the memory of my beloved companions who have crossed the Rainbow Bridge throughout the years. They hold a special place in my heart: TC, Nureyev, Barishnikiov, Tammy, Bubbles, Fiona, Emma, and Greta. Tragically, two of them were victims of hit-and-run accidents. Emma developed a mass on her stomach, leading me to make the heart-wrenching decision to let her go. Fiona, too, reached a point where I had to make the same painful choice. Tammy, the one pictured in a Halloween costume, passed away right beside me on my bed. Bubbles left us unexpectedly before I returned home from work one fateful day. These incredible beings lived long lives, with most of the girls being between 17 to 20 years old when they departed. Greta, the youngest at only 5 months, had an allergic reaction to anaesthesia and peacefully passed away in my arms at the vet's office. Their absence is felt deeply, and I carry the love and memories of each of them in my heart, missing them dearly.

The Endless Litterbox

A car narrowly missed me, swerving and hooting. The huge, noisy machine was terrifying, but it brought me to my senses. I knew I would have to be more careful if *she* was going to find me alive this time around, so I exercised the utmost discretion and stuck to the gutters, staying out of the way as best I could. I traversed the unfamiliar streets, crouching low each time a car came past and willing the occupants to *not* notice me.

An unfamiliar salty smell pervaded the air all around me. It wasn't unpleasant and instinct told me I'd be safer closer to its source, so I made my way across several garden fences until I found an unoccupied house to hide beneath until nightfall. The young couple searched up and down the streets of the neighbourhood calling for "Robby", but I wasn't him. I refused to answer to anything except my own name. Truth be told, I had resolved never to answer to any human ever again – except *her*, the one to whom I belonged.

When darkness eventually fell, I explored the garden next door. I was wary of it because it smelled strongly of dog and I didn't have much reason to trust them. Dogs usually mean danger. It was pitch dark and silent. Keeping a cautious eye out, I searched for an easy meal. Dogs were nowhere to be seen, but I couldn't find anything to eat. There was a little pool in the shrubbery beside a bench in a quiet corner of the garden and I drank deeply from the cool, delicious water. The day had been hot and my headlong flight had left my throat parched.

I lifted my nose up and got a good fix on the scent filling the air and decided to go in search of it. I took some wrong turns and had to backtrack, all the while avoiding houses where there was the odour of dogs. Annoyingly, most of these dog houses also smelled of food and I could no longer ignore the rumbling in my belly. I hopped onto a low fence and immediately spotted a dog asleep on the deck of a large house in a lush garden. Just beyond the slumbering beast was a bowl with the remains of its evening meal. The fat canine had evidently had its fill and insects were buzzing industriously around the remnants. I dropped down from the fence stealthily, landing as silently as I could. Eyeing the dog and poised to flee instantly, I steeled my nerves but it slept on, snoring asthmatically, strings of greenish, yellow drool hanging from its jowls.

I crept onto the deck. One careful foot at a time, I slunk up to the bowl and froze. He stirred but was still asleep. No one was about. Within seconds I had devoured the dregs of the dog's dinner, but I was far from satisfied. I left the garden as quietly as I had entered and moved on to the next target. This one was not as promising. When I leapt onto the fence, the resident dogs kicked up such a din that I fled like a wraith into the night. But I didn't give up. I was still hungry, so went looking for another dog to steal from. I squeezed between the slats of a wooden fence where I could smell dogs and food, but I wasn't able to see them. Cautiously, I made my way around to the back of the house where I found some dogs who had just been served their evening meal. They were devouring it eagerly. My mouth watered as I watched them lick up every morsel, leaving not a smear of gravy behind. Disappointed, I slipped back into the shadows before I was detected. I explored my options in several more gardens before giving up.

In the light of the rising sun, I crossed Centennial Drive and entered the narrow green belt which fringes the New Plymouth coastline. The fresh breeze sighed through the bushes while I enjoyed the sensation of rotting leaves and humus under my paws. It was cool and pleasant here, unlike the unforgiving tarmac of people streets. The sight that met my eyes as I summited a shallow sandy dune is one I'll never forget. Ahead lay the most extensive strip of sand I had ever seen. It stretched as far as the eye could see, left and right. It wasn't very broad, and beyond it to the North-West were the great waters of the North Taranaki Bight. I have since learned that people call this gigantic pool with no visible boundaries "the sea" or "the ocean", and that sand is what they call "a beach". In my ignorance, it was simply the biggest toilet I had laid eyes on, but I soon learned there was a lot more to it. I discovered that it was not really the most suitable litterbox. Its sand had a salty tang which, when I washed my paws after walking on it, left an intense aftertaste that made me thirsty. Nevertheless, on that fine, quiet morning, I explored the beach thoroughly, careful not to venture close to the noisy water slopping perpetually at its edge. It was too early for any people to be about which suited me fine. There were all manner of things washed up in heaps, including a man-made object that looked quite lethal: a vicious curved hook attached to fine, plastic string. There were salt-encrusted pieces of wood, shells of interesting-smelling creatures and rotting pieces of the most fascinating plants I had ever seen, all permeated by the pungent odour of fish.

Some of my finds seemed edible. There was half a fish and a strange crusty looking creature with way too many legs but which smelt palatable. Several of the shells had peculiar-smelling contents which might have been OK to eat, but I wasn't sure. My nose is usually very sensitive and lets me know if what I'm about to eat is still good, but the overpowering smell of fish was dulling it. Nevertheless, I was so hungry that I started nibbling at the fish carcass and followed up by licking out the slimy contents of some of the shells.

The Good Samaritan

Later that day, as I lay napping in the cool of the vegetation at the edge of the beach, I became aware of a slight discomfort in my belly. I felt nauseous and not entirely well. It wasn't too bad, so I shook my head and tried to ignore it. I was thirsty but knew better than to venture near the seething water at the shoreline. I would have to find water elsewhere. Also, I knew I would probably feel better if I ate something solid and familiar. A fat blackbird was perched sleepily on a low branch immediately above me. I eyed her critically, formulating a strategy, but I really wasn't hungry enough to try and catch her. She would have been an easy one, but I found I had no appetite. I heaved myself to my feet and wandered around listlessly, uncertain. I began to feel steadily worse. I knew I needed water urgently and, by the time night fell, I was distinctly unwell. I made my way back across Centennial Drive by the light of the moon, seeking hydration.

Eventually I found a house with a large built-in water bowl positioned under its garden tap, presumably for its canine or feline residents. I was past caring as I slaked my raging thirst and crept into a nearby bed of petunias to sleep. I turned around a few times, trampling the foliage into a comfortable nest before flopping down and curling myself into a tight ball. It was a warm late-October evening, but I felt cold and sick. Tremors rocked my little body during the night as the illness took hold. I left my bed several times during the night to slake the persistent thirst. Before sunrise, I sat miserably in the flowerbed as spasm after spasm wracked my exhausted body. There was nothing in my stomach left to bring up, and it was all I could do to stumble out of the garden, back into the safety of the bush across the road. I remained in the coastal vegetation for the entire day, too weak to move. The short distance to my ready source of fresh water was too far for me.

By late afternoon, I was delirious. From the depths of a deep, dark tunnel, I was aware of sounds. A remnant of my self-preservation forced me to my feet and I tried to run. I fell forward onto my face and then everything went dark. I drifted in and out of consciousness, oblivious to my surroundings, resigned to my fate.

Kindness reflects the value of the giver, not the recipient.

Never waste an opportunity to be kind.

I no longer cared about anything. Each time I let myself float up... up... up... towards the light which would liberate me, a tentative force reached out and pulled me gently back. I have no idea how long I was in this state, nor how I escaped detection by human or dog, but I gradually began feeling better and my consciousness returned. The vile pathogen which had poisoned my system must have eventually run its course and worked its way out of me. I positively reeked. The stench of my own vomit and diarrhoea was unbearable. I crept away from the contaminated site after first attempting to cover the mess, but I didn't have the strength to move even a twig.

Miraculously, I made it back to the house with the water where I drank deeply and felt somewhat revived. I was too weak to hunt, so I remained hidden under the shrubs. There were no dogs or cats on the premises as I had first thought. The kind

man who lived here simply filled the bowl every day with fresh water for the birds and beasties who visited his garden. I stayed out of sight as he came and went. He looked in my direction often, but I remained hidden as he went about his business. At the end of my second day there, I noticed that a bowl of kitty biscuits had appeared at the back door. I assumed this meal was meant for me. I was ravenous now that I was feeling better although still not capable of catching anything, so I fell upon the biscuits with relish and sent him thoughts of gratitude.

The Snare

I remained there for a few days regaining my strength, grateful for the provisions of the Good Samaritan but unwilling to allow him near. He tried quite hard to befriend me, and I'm ashamed to say I was rather rude. I hissed at him when he approached, and he got the message to leave me be. I was in no mood for another cage and further disappointment at the hands of people.

When I was fully recovered, I managed to catch a huge rat I had been observing for some time. It had gnawed a hole in the weatherboard behind a clump of azaleas growing against the wall underneath the kitchen window and came and went from its nest under the house through this hole at will. I lay in wait for it. I was tempted to eat it myself but left it on my host's doorstep as a parting gift in appreciation of his kindness towards me. Yes, yes, I know! Humans don't eat rats. For some reason though, they love it when cats gift them with dead ones.

With a cool evening breeze carrying the scent of the sea, I turned my back on that garden and its prospect of a comfortable life. Crossing Centennial Drive was tricky, and I narrowly missed being run over as I made several attempts at it. Then I was safely across and in the relative sanctuary of the green belt. It was to be an adventure-filled night. First, I stumbled upon a trio of stoned teenagers in the low dunes. I emerged from a narrow track in the bushes straight into the midst of their covert gathering where they were lying motionless in a glassy-eyed stupor. My sudden appearance startled them enough that they gathered their few

A good guest leaves memories that can be treasured forever.

It was the fish-flavoured cat food I'd been fed as a special treat when I lived at the shop, but there was a smell of decay layered over it. I followed my nose. Traps for stoats, weasels, possums, and other small animals considered pests are often baited with cat food and set in places frequented by cats, near pathways and roadsides, stream margins and at the edges of human habitat. Humans are indiscriminate killers. Had there not been the stench of a dead animal already caught in that trap, I might very well have been tempted to stick my paw in and have a wee taste. I recoiled in horror when I recognised the remains of another cat: one who hadn't been as fortunate as I. The poor creature had probably suffered a painful and prolonged death in a trap designed to kill smaller animals immediately, but which could also ensnare a cat without the mercy of instant death. I was badly shaken and added another mental note to my long list of reasons to mistrust people.

remaining wits and came after me, but their clumsy, troll-like efforts were futile and I outsmarted them easily. Several minutes later, I could still hear them crashing through the brush trying to find me.

Then, as I trotted into the darkness on silent paws, I became aware of a strong, fishy smell, far more intense than the sea. I recognised it immediately.

"Of all the creatures that were made, man is the most detestable. Of the entire brood he is the only one - the solitary one - that possesses malice. That is the basest of all instincts, passions, vices-the most hateful. He is the only creature that has pain for sport, knowing it to be pain."

- Mark Twain's Autobiography

The Fringe of Civilisation

Over the next few weeks, I got to know the green belt strip and its adjacent industrial area below Paritutu Rock very well. I had become wary of traffic after several near misses crossing the busy roads. Badly shaken one afternoon after an encounter with an eighteen-wheeler, I crawled into a storage area at the back of a factory and made myself comfortable amongst the big blue chemical barrels and some interesting-smelling cardboard boxes. I waited out the last few hours of daylight there, dozing lightly until the sun sank below the horizon in a blaze of gold, orange, and pink.

I heard the distant sounds of humans leaving, roller doors closing. Someone walked past the entrance to my storage bay and then was gone. All the lights went off with a snap and silence descended over the factory. I waited five minutes, making sure there were no humans left and then came out of hiding. At one end of the gigantic floor-space were the rubbish bins, standing in a line next to a large metal roller door. I approached them quietly, sniffed around in likely places and quickly picked up the scent of mice and rats! I leapt up onto the low wall behind the row of bins, crouched down and waited.

It wasn't long before a foraging party of three mice put in an appearance at the edge of the untidy pile of litter, investigating discarded plastic bags and containers before settling on the mouldy remains of some sandwiches. They began to feed, unaware of the danger lurking in the shadows above.

I shifted into position and prepared to strike. With every muscle tensed and ready, I selected my target and launched at the group from the parapet. My forepaws were closing around my intended victim before she even felt the rush of wind my body had displaced. The other two fled, squealing in terror. I administered a swift bite to the back of her neck. The mouse twitched and went still. I was no fat, bored housecat. I was a hunter killing to survive. I devoured her in seconds, her leathery tail the only remaining proof of her existence. She had been a plump one, but I was still hungry.

My chance of a second kill in this spot was slim. The vermin would be overly cautious now that they knew I was on the prowl, and I would be wasting my time lying in wait here. I cleaned myself up quickly, making sure that my paws and whiskers were free from all traces of blood, trotted off and let myself out of the factory. I squeezed through the slats of a wooden fence and found myself in a neighbouring section. On high alert for guard dogs and other dangers, I started sniffing around but all I found was a mountain of discarded tyres and motorcar entrails. After a thorough investigation of the junkyard, I concluded that there were no easy pickings to be had here and moved on.

At last, I found what I was looking for: a human eatery. It was a corner dairy which served coffee and light meals, all shut up for the night. I knew what was likely to be at the back if I could just get over the wall. With an almighty leap, I managed to reach the top where I teetered for a moment to regain my balance. I steadied myself with a grace and finesse that can only be achieved by cats and dropped silently down the other side. As I had expected, there was an overflowing bin in the corner of the yard. It was the setting for a veritable party as multiple foraging night-creatures tucked into their meal of stale chips, breadcrusts, pie-crumbs and other scraps which had been discarded by wasteful humans.

My hunting skills were improving by the day, and while I was becoming less reliant on manmade provisions, I found the messy habits of people quite useful. Wherever they were, they left rubbish which in turn lured the creatures upon which I preyed. I carefully assessed my position. I wouldn't be able to make a successful catch from my current location. If I charged the bin head on, they would see me coming and scatter. I jumped back onto the wall and padded quietly along the top, calculating the best angle of attack. My prey were still blissfully unaware of me and focussing on the contents of the bin. The best approach would be to stalk them from the rear, and I crouched down on my belly as low as I could go, inching my way the last few metres in slow motion with the fluid grace of a leopard approaching an unsuspecting gazelle.

I surveyed the choices with the practised ease of a sniper dialling in his night-sight and selected a large rat on the periphery. I waited for the right moment, every muscle coiled and ready, and… there it was: the rat put his head down to pick up a chunk of pie crust. I launched myself at him from above and behind. In a trice, he was dead and hanging limply in my jaws. Rats are dangerous prey, and no mistake. They fight back if the kill is not a clean one and can inflict serious injuries with their sharp, filthy teeth.

I stood for a moment on the tower of refuse spilling from the bin, gloating with my conquest in my mouth, then leapt down and trotted off, triumphant. I couldn't feast on the rat in this dingy courtyard. Rats are intelligent creatures, capable of organising to gang up on a lone cat, and the bolder ones here may have sought immediate revenge. There were certainly a lot of them in this place. If I was a lion in the feral jungle at the fringes of human civilisation, then you could say that rats were its hyenas. I couldn't risk being cornered by an army of them, so, with the dead rat dangling from my mouth, I hastily clawed my way back up the wall. The remaining rats regrouped into an angry, chittering melee below. I left before they decided to swarm up after me and dropped to the dairy's forecourt, landing squarely on my feet.

I moved rapidly away from the scene of the crime and sought out a tree in the concrete wasteland. A lonely Pohutukawa, out of place in the man-made abomination, appeared in the darkness ahead and I made a beeline for it. I settled into the elbow of a thick branch after judging it a defensible position and dined like a king, savouring every salty morsel. Being a proper cat, I had a long wash afterwards. I spent time ensuring each whisker was spotless. These sensitive antennae on my face and the back of my legs, above my paws, were crucial to my survival, and I had to ensure their precise maintenance. I cleaned each claw, picking out the remnants of flesh and fur with my teeth and polishing them with my rough tongue. When I was done, it was time to exercise. I stood on tiptoe and arched my back as far as it would go, then reached forward with my front legs and elevated my rear as high as I could. I held this graceful, curved arch for a few moments, maximising the stretch until my muscles ached, then flexed my claws, digging them rapidly in and out of the rough bark, purring with satisfaction as I sharpened the tools of my trade.

After a long and productive night, I was now ready for sleep. The denizens of my tree were beginning to stir, puffing out their chests and clearing their throats, readying themselves for their dawn chorus in which they would bear witness to the end of another dangerous night. I turned in earlier than usual and, as the birds began their song to welcome the new day, I fell into a deep sleep, curled into a tight ball in my comfortable cradle.

The search begins again

In late November, news broke that I had escaped again. By this time I had already been living rough for more than a month in New Plymouth. Christmas came and went. In the world of humans, Covid-19 was stilll the big talking point at the end of 2020; consequently, not many people cared about a missing cat, just one of so many. Thankfully, there were those who never gave up on me. They went back to the drawing board and started their search from scratch.

* 24 November 2020 - The McDonnells organise and distribute flyers, for the second search. The media is alerted. Traps, trail cams etc. are arranged. Volunteers led by Bobbie Johnson go door to door in search of Rodney.
* December 2020 - Various possible sightings at multiple locations. All leads followed up by the volunteer team but Rodney remains elusive.
* January 2021 - Further sightings throughout the month, mostly at industrial sites and properties backing onto the green belt.
* 9 February 2021 - Very probable sighting on a vacant property below Paritutu Rock.
* 14 February 2021 - Cameras set up on the vacant section. Results indicate that the stray is almost certainly Rodney.

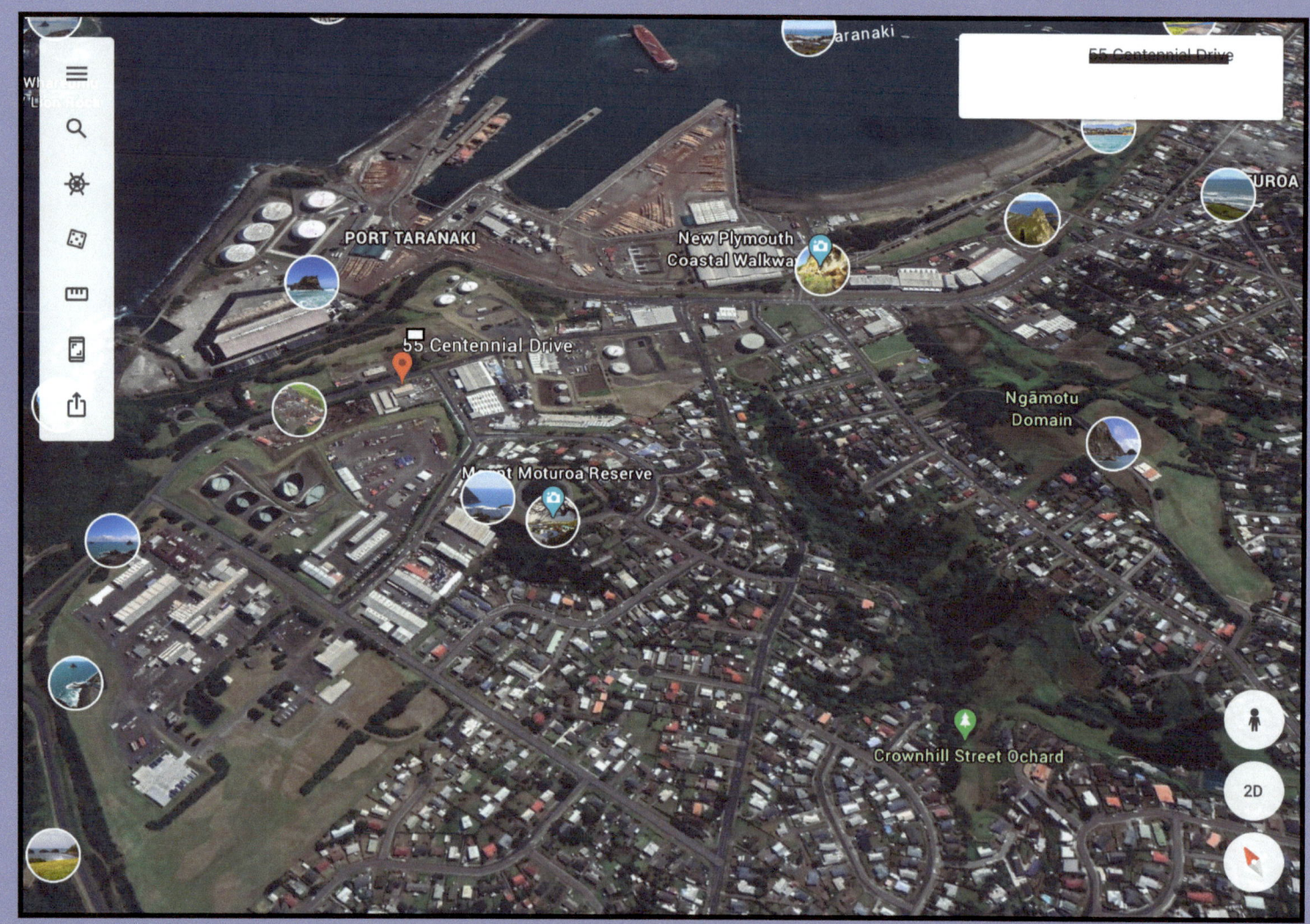

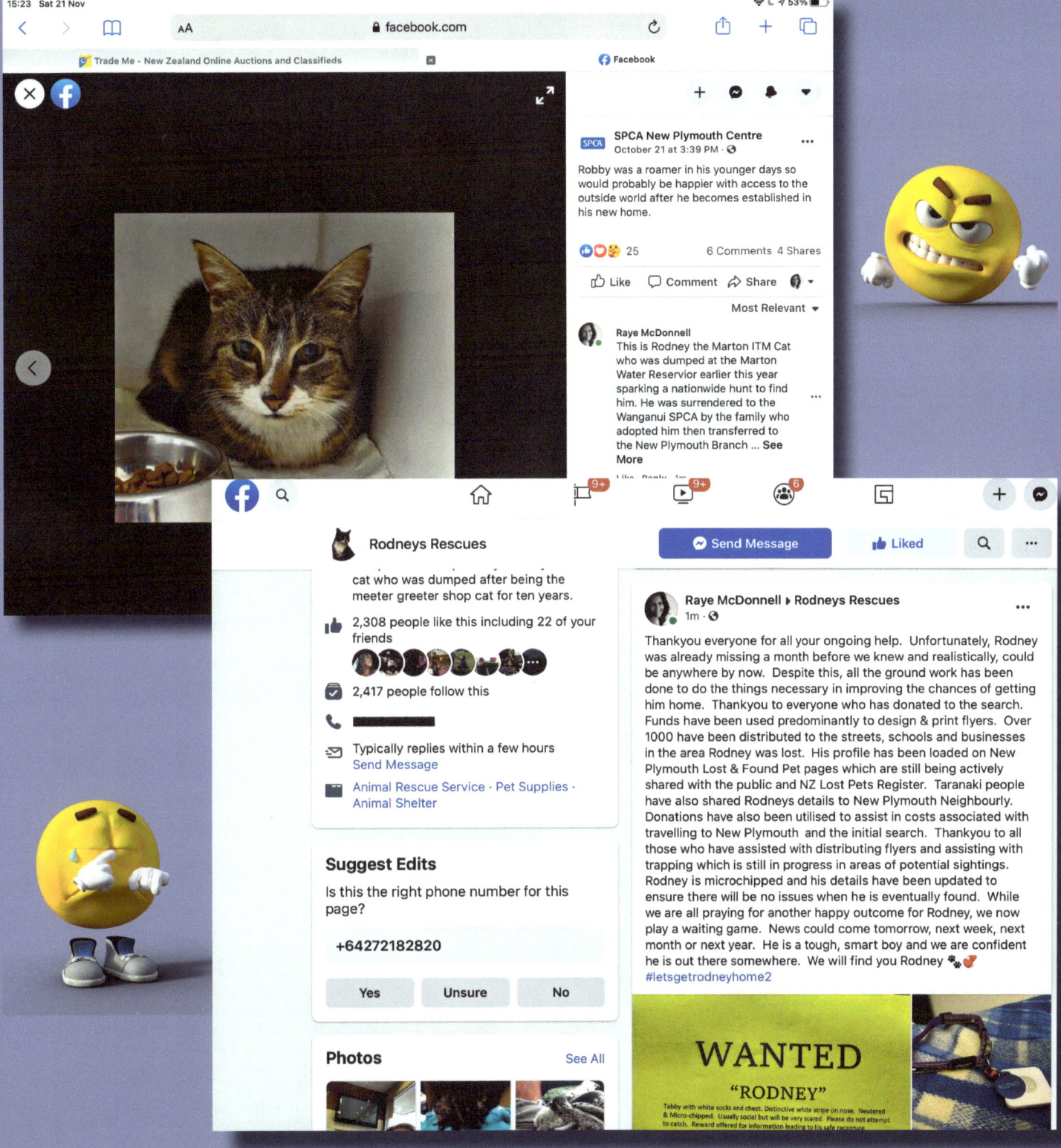

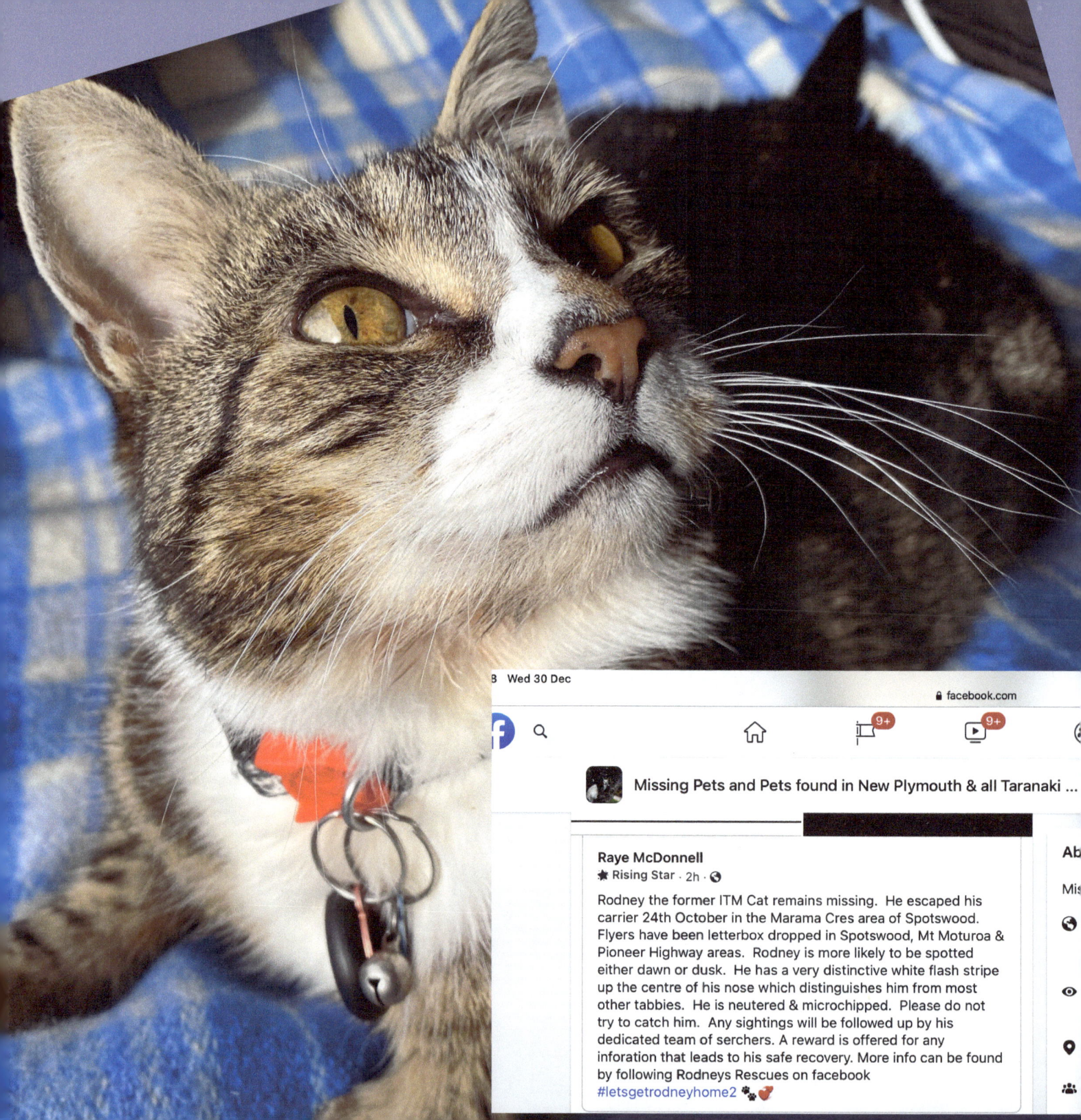

If you don't get lost, you may never be found.

 **Rodneys Rescues**
 Public

We have had positive sightings in Paritutu Rd, Herekawe Dr, Tahurangi Pl & possible sightings in both Pomare Pl & Tohora Pl. Rodney has a special fondness for woodpiles and workmen having being raised in a lumberyard. If you have woodpiles/rubbish piles or a shed on your property and are in the area of Rodney sightings, please keep an eye out for him. Rodney is a thickly striped, darker tabby cat with a very distinctive white flash stripe up his nose which distinguishes him from other tabby cats. He is more likely to be spotted early morning (dawn) or evening (dusk). We know Rodney is alive and still in the area & that flyer drops (Thankyou Team Bobbie) are working. All it will take is that one phone call to get him home 🐾💗

Cat Fight

I survived all that Summer by frequenting derelict buildings and human businesses to get my food by night, then disappearing like a phantom into the green belt to rest up during the day. I saw very few humans close up except once when a man who was working late emerged suddenly from a site office and lit up a smoke. He was temporarily blinded by

the brightness of the flame and stumbled over me as he came down the steps of the prefab building where I was crouched in deep concentration prospecting for mice. A string of expletives escaped his pinched mouth but despite this, the cigarette dangling from his lips remained in place. I meowed apologetically but was rewarded with a swift kick aimed at my head which I dodged easily. I beat a hasty retreat and resolved not to be caught off guard again.

I avoided humans and dogs but was also leery of contact with my own kind. Many feral cats lived in the shadows between buildings of the industrial area, and they too fought for survival, heavily reliant on the vermin attracted by human activity.

It was inevitable that I would sometimes come into contact with another cat doing it tough, and I managed these encounters by adopting a non-threatening stance, staying well out of reach which was usually sufficient to avoid bloodshed.

I had my first and only serious cat fight at the far end of Breakwater Road, near the docks. One night, I innocently wandered into a narrow alleyway in search of food. I knew that these dockside cats were the toughest of the tough. They had been born into this hostile environment and were fully adapted to it. Some had worked out the value of cooperation and banded together in loosely associated gangs to aid their survival. It was a dangerous area, but I was hungry.

realised my mistake as soon as I entered. Around me, silent witnesses crouched in the shadows observing dispassionately as the drama was about to unfold in front of them. These were the flotsam and jetsam of human callousness: the abandoned, unwanted, and rejected. A few of them had been in a predicament similar to mine and had turned feral; others had been born in human homes but dumped - barely weaned - to make it on their own or die. Most had been born wild. They were all survivors having fought for every fragment of their precarious existence. These hostile cats around me, perched on top of log piles and strategic vantage points had no intention of sharing their turf with an interloper

A new arrival had to earn his place in the colony. I was nervous but they made no move - yet - keeping a watchful eye on me. I hung back. Wary. Vigilant. As always, unwilling to initiate confrontation.

The first attack came from a young tabby. Although I'd been living rough for a while, I was much larger and healthier than the average, undernourished, parasite-infested feral cat. I was also quite fit from all my recent exercise. He was barely a challenge, and I managed to get the upper paw by pouncing on him and delivering a stinging blow with razor-sharp claws unsheathed to their

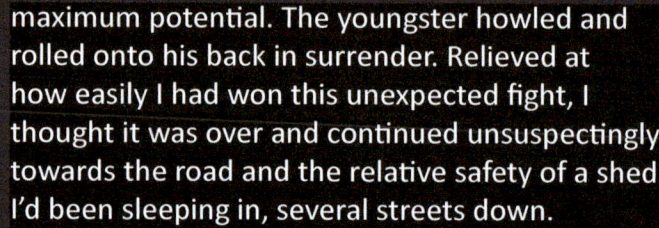

maximum potential. The youngster howled and rolled onto his back in surrender. Relieved at how easily I had won this unexpected fight, I thought it was over and continued unsuspectingly towards the road and the relative safety of a shed I'd been sleeping in, several streets down.

But I was not going to be let off that easily. I had inadvertently trespassed into the territory of a scrawny old black Tom, the alpha male of the feral colony. The inexperienced tabby had presumably been one of his offspring. I knew that further conflict was unavoidable and I steeled my nerves in preparation. Suddenly, all hell broke loose. Cats appeared directly ahead. I turned and ran but my escape was cut off by two more cats who emerged from the shadows beneath the wall. I was trapped. My only option was to fight!

One of the cats advanced, back arched, fur puffed up. He was howling an unearthly shriek designed to strike terror into my heart. My own tail fluffed up to three times its usual girth and the hair on my back stood in a straight ridge. I laid my ears back flat and issued my own bloodcurdling battle cry. I may have been a reluctant warrior, but I was no coward – I was not going down without a fight. Adrenaline flooded my system. I would fight to the death if necessary. I hissed back at my attacker, baring sharp fangs. His amber eyes flashed angrily. I dared him to strike first.

It was the black Tom. He approached inch by inch, head low and back arched. He maintained his banshee-like screaming as all the others hung back. We circled in a fearful dance, sizing each other up. I was by far the larger. My ten-year, high-protein diet gave me advantages of size and strength, but he was a cunning, experienced scrapper, a veteran of many battles. He had territory and a harem to defend. This was no minor squabble. It would probably end in death for one of us.

The black Tom hissed and spat angrily, calling me out. I restrained myself, still unwilling to be the instigator. I had retreated from his territory at the first opportunity, but I was certainly prepared to defend myself. In the end, I had no option. With a howl of testosterone-fuelled rage, he launched his attack. We lunged and swiped at each other with fang and claw, screaming and tumbling, crashing into walls and pavement. I dodged most of his blows, but a lightning-fast claw suddenly raked across my face – narrowly missing an eye – and ripped a sliver out of my ear. I felt the stinging pain and retaliated with a powerful blow of my own, then somersaulted clear of his potent back legs which were trying to rake at my soft underbelly. Fur flew in every direction and our blood sprayed the dirty walls and floor of the alley. Then we were in a hate-filled embrace as each tried to deliver the killing bite. I tore myself free just as his jaws snapped closed on the empty air where my throat had been a split second ago.

He was emboldened by my defensive tactics and stormed me again, but I refused to concede. I was in a desperate situation. I continued fighting back. Most of it was fuelled by adrenaline, but there was something else. Deep inside, I found a reservoir of strength and the courage to fight on. I had to survive for *her*.

He drew his head back arrogantly, confidently, in preparation for the killing blow. In that moment, I struck one of my own. Quick as a snake, I had him by the throat and clamped down hard. I felt my jaws crunch through skin, flesh and cartilage and bore down with all my might. My teeth punctured his trachea and I squeezed even harder, cutting off his air supply. He flailed wildly, raking at me with his back claws and tearing a huge gash in my flank despite the protection of my thick fur, but I clung on, the pain urging me to bite down tighter and tighter.

His thrashing weakened and then stopped. Finally, I let go. His blood oozed out over the grey earth as his life ebbed away. The fight had been brutal but had lasted only a minute. Silence fell over the audience as I challenged them. They had been the aggressors a few moments ago, but now they assumed defensive poses and submitted to me one by one before slinking away. His squad had consisted mainly of females who either rolled over and exposed their bellies or slumped with their shoulders to the ground. Some merely drifted away avoiding eye contact. The law of the jungle had prevailed. I was the survivor and now the alpha cat.

It was not a responsibility I wanted. I was weary and wounded. Above all, I wanted to be left alone to assess my injuries, lick my wounds and sleep. I was not even hungry any more. I limped over to a derelict shed nearby. One of its double doors was slumped on a rusty hinge, the other long since claimed by the elements and was nowhere to be seen. Some cats followed submissively at a safe distance, but most of them had melted away into the night. The shed smelled strongly of cat urine and, as I entered, I identified the pheromones of the black Tom I had killed. At the back, I found a stack of wooden crates, rotten and fragile, on top of which was a pile of rags that reeked of my adversary. I crawled tiredly onto the filthy rags and claimed my throne. My new lieutenants would take care of things while I slept, just as they had done for my predecessor.

Sometimes you have to fight for something you never lost.

Rainbow Bridge Tributes

Casper & Daniel by Annette Gentry

Two of the most endearing fur babies I've ever had the privilege of knowing. I hope you're enjoying watching the birds in heaven. I miss you every single day and hold onto my love for you eternally. I look forward to the day we'll reunite at the Rainbow Bridge.

Gracie by Neil Longbottom

Gracie, my very first rescue kitty, set me on the path to becoming a devoted Crazy Cat Dad (a Russian Blue and a DSH tabby kitten later). Abandoned after her previous owner departed without settling her rent, she became my world for three precious years. I was grateful to provide her with a warm and comfortable home until she sadly crossed the Bridge due to an ear disease. Rest peacefully, Princess.

Fenway by Denise Scott

Fenway came into the world from a feral Momma kitty on 4/7/2013. Thankfully, a friend managed to trap the Momma cat (who continues to live with our friend) and provided her babies, including Fenway, a good start in life. However, we later discovered that he had a severe heart murmur, and the vet suggested putting him down.

Refusing to give up, I sought the expertise of a specialist for Fenway. With exceptional care, he lived a remarkably happy life despite the initial prognosis.

He was an incredibly affectionate, tender, and gentle kitty, though he possessed the spirit of a true alpha cat, ruling his Cat Kingdom with grace. On pleasant days, he relished sitting out on the deck, basking in the warmth of the sun. On Sunday, February 11, 2018, as I returned home from church, he approached me, visibly distressed, crying and struggling to breathe.

It was his time. With tender, soothing words and a prolonged, affectionate embrace, he peacefully crossed over the Rainbow Bridge.

Pandora by Dave Aceves

Pandora was initially a stray, but I was allowed to rescue her. She was discovered in the fields of Northern California, where the landowner threatened to shoot her because of her diarrhoea. She tested positive for FIV, and while vets recommended euthanasia, her vitality and overall health convinced us otherwise. Initially quite skittish, she transformed into the gentlest kitty, living seven joyful years with us. She adored being a lap cat and exploring, navigating our home more than any other cat. Her daily adventures were her trademark. Unfortunately, she battled cancer, becoming an oncology patient for six months. Initially responding well to chemotherapy, her condition deteriorated in the last month. She grew weak, lost weight, and couldn't partake in her usual explorations. Eventually, it was time. She spent her final days on her warmer bed, purring as we comforted her. With the aid of a home vet, she peacefully passed away in our arms.

We miss her dearly, and the ache in our hearts continues, reminiscing about the wonderful memories. Pandy, you are deeply loved and missed every day.

Izzie by Cushla Astorga

In 2021, Izzie journeyed across the Rainbow Bridge. She was not just a pet but my familiar, always by my side and my loyal foot warmer. She held a special place in my heart. Surviving her first stroke in September 2020 was a testament to her resilience, but sadly, she endured a second stroke six months later. With heavy hearts, we bid our goodbyes and assisted her in crossing the rainbow bridge at the age of 14. I deeply miss her presence every day.

The Colony

I woke when filtered sunlight streamed through the high, dirty windows. Mesmerised by swirling dust motes, I lay in the slanting rays until I remembered where I was. I was stiff and sore from the fight, my every movement painful. I sat and began the long task of cleaning myself up. To add to my torment, I was covered in fleas from the infested bedding and no matter how I scratched, I could get no relief from the determined parasites. I was stumbling down from the wooden stack to get away from them when I saw a pair of green eyes belonging to a small, tortoiseshell cat tracking me from a safe distance. We regarded each other in silence for a minute, then I simply ignored her and set about tending to my wounds. Many of the scratches crisscrossing my body didn't concern me: they were shallow and would scab over and heal, as would my torn ear. The deep gash on my leg was another matter entirely. It was extremely painful and impairing my movement.

I counted myself lucky to have avoided those lethal, dirty fangs. Cat bites - just like human bites for that matter - are deadly. Deep puncture wounds leave bacteria trapped in the tissue and almost always result in an abscess which, if not treated and drained, can poison with deadly infection. It is often the case that secondary bacterial infection kills when the bite itself is not fatal.

The Tortoiseshell approached me respectfully, carrying something in her mouth. I kept one eye on her as I continued my self-ministrations. She halted just out of reach, dropped a half-eaten mouse at my

feet, then retreated hastily. I sniffed at her peace offering and accepted it magnanimously. I wasn't particularly hungry, but I nibbled at it to show appreciation. It was the first of many. In the days that followed, the rest of the clan paid homage in various ways, but I had little interest in being their leader. I had a single purpose: I wanted to be with *her*, and I knew *she* would be coming for me.

As pets, we form close associations with humans. I don't know why, but we cats prefer human companionship to that of our own kind. Our dignity and sense of self-worth is often interpreted as aloofness by those who don't know better, but there is no questioning our love for our humans. We don't wear our hearts on our sleeves, and we have too much self-respect to grovel for attention or food, both of which are rightfully due to us. We expect these things to be offered freely in equal partnership, and we provide company and friendship in return. It is a relationship of mutual respect, not one of subservience nor of co-dependency. Following my extremely sociable life in the shop, I chose a solitary existence after the betrayal, yet I held firm to the belief that my destiny was always going to be with a human companion.

When forced to live outside the circle of human friendship, cats sometimes band together in colonies. Such cats are labelled 'feral'.

Some cats can survive on their own if forced, but it is a miserable existence and they won't live long. As a result, most will gravitate towards a colony where each cat remains the master of its own destiny but cooperates with the others for a better chance at survival. Feral queens often leave kittens in the care of others when hunting and share the spoils on their return. They often feed each other's kittens. Cats understand the concept of family very well indeed.

I could have taken over this colony and stayed, but I knew this life was not for me. Sooner or later, I would be challenged and pay the ultimate price. I hadn't asked for this responsibility or the fight that had precipitated it, but I remained in the relative safety of the colony while I healed. They knew where there were easy meals to be had. They tore open rubbish bags and fed from the bins behind restaurants and shops, and hunted vermin competing for these pickings. Fights often broke out for the choicest bits, but I hung back, never claiming what was rightfully mine. I kept my interaction with the aggressive cats to a minimum and relied on my temporary notoriety within the colony, biding my time. Whenever they squabbled over the scraps from restaurant tables, I lurked in the shadows instead, picking off mice and rats at the periphery who were just waiting their turn. By the time the cats dragged their tasty morsels off, my hunger was already sated, and I'd scatter the hesitating mice to give the bins a once-over. There was never much left for me, but it was plenty for the rats and mice who were lower in the food chain and did not mind vegetarian meals. I asserted my dominance over them as a game, daring them to scramble up while I held the position of power on top of the bin, while all they could do was glare and squeak from a safe distance.

Eye On The Prize

It was a relatively easy and comfortable source of food, but I didn't want to stay too long. As soon as my wounds were sufficiently healed, I made up my mind to abandon my charges. My emotions were the same as those experienced by humans when inadvertently harming another. I had no intention of killing the black cat. Up until then, I had killed only to avoid starvation or to serve my humans. He had given me no choice but to defend myself and, unluckily for him, had paid the price. Had I not won, I would have paid with my own life. When I left, there would be a power vacuum, followed by another fight for dominance and the position of leader would be decided very quickly. I found I hated this filthy part of town, teeming with its many people and their noisy machines. I had frequented it only for its readily available food-sources and had witnessed first-hand the discarded, forgotten ferals it had sucked into its orbit. They were a sad indictment on humanity's arrogant, selfish abuse of their environment.

I pondered these things in a typically feline way; not in verbal thought or concrete images as humans might do, but instinctively. Vague feelings swam mistily through my mind and deep within my being, none of which could be explained by simple nerve impulses or neural connections. The paradox did not escape me: a growing mistrust and contempt for humans was in direct contrast to my overwhelming need to be with *her*. I needed to be found so that I could be claimed by the one human who was destined to be mine.

Found ! (Again.)

17 February 2021 - A microchip scan provides confirmation that the cat caught in one of the traps is indeed Rodney. He is formally adopted by Raye and Shane in Whanganui and handed over to them to live the rest of his days in peace and comfort.

Some of the places I got to know very well during my four month stay in New Plymouth.

I watched the sunrise on 17th February 2021 and then walked away from the colony. I made my way to a spot I'd used before: a vacant lot adjacent to Paritutu Rock. It had a grassy meadow, covered in dandelions. There was a shed in one corner and an old camper van in the other. I liked

this location very much. It was a peaceful one, but close enough to my productive hunting grounds.

I was sitting under the weed-entangled lavender bush one morning, grooming my whiskers when a pair of mice unexpectedly scurried out from under the leaves of the Kawakawa. I wasn't particularly hungry, but they triggered a primal urge in me, so I crouched down low and inched forward towards them. Their smell was tantalising, and I made some involuntary chittering sounds as my jaw trembled. One of the rodents spotted me and froze. Its partner saw me too and fled for its life. For the simple challenge of it, I chose the one already in full retreat and took off after it.

Despite the head start, it was no match for my experience and the chase was over in seconds. I pounced, snapping its neck with my powerful forepaws. Because I wasn't hungry, I toyed with the dead creature for a while, tossing it into the air and catching it, exercising my muscles. Then, mindful that my next meal was never guaranteed, I ate it.

I was taking a catnap under the camper van to aid my digestion when my psychic antennae began to tingle. My ears twitched. I turned them this way and that, my physical senses hunting for something I already knew from a level deeper than instinct. Someone who cares about animals had entered my territory. From my safe vantage behind the axle, I homed in on the woman in my field. She was huffing and puffing in the hot sun, lugging heavy traps about in the long grass and setting them up in the shade under trees and bushes.

I had sensed her before. She had been with *her* many months ago as I ran from the woodpile at the dam. She finally withdrew, leaving the metal boxes behind. I knew what they were, and recalled the anguish of the cat trapped at the woodpile.

I smelled the delicious food left inside the traps but I sat all afternoon, merely observing. I knew what I had to do. Feral cats should stay away from traps, but I was not feral and tempting as it was, the food held no great attraction for me. I could fend for myself. A spell seemed to have been cast on me though, compelling me to walk towards the nearest box. Curiosity did not kill the cat in this instance – I walked into the trap voluntarily, sure in the knowledge that it would transport me to *her*.
Her. *Raye*, my forever human. And as I wished it, so it was to be.

Sunrise on the morning that I finally came home to her, Raye.

Home At Last

At first, I was a little nervous in the car. My previous experience in cars hadn't been positive, but I knew I was going to my forever home this time, with my mum, Raye, so I settled down and slept for most of the journey to Whanganui. We arrived at Santo Stables at 11:30PM on Wednesday, 17th February 2021.

Mum settled me into my crate and gave me a warm, comfortable bed – the first in many months. She also made sure I went to bed on a full tummy. She says that she and Dad got very little sleep that night because they kept checking in on me to see if I was alright; also to make sure I wasn't just a dream and that I really was finally home. Home! Where I belonged.

The following morning, I greeted Mum and Dad with lots of chirps and head-butts because I was so pleased to be with them. It was a relief to know that I was safe and cared for at last. I hardly ever meow, but I am a very vocal, chirpy chatter and talk to Mum in this way all the time.

I had Mum and Dad trained very quickly. They are fast learners! For example, they now know I love to have the sides of my face rubbed and scratched right up to my ears. I can't get enough of this! It feels nice but, more importantly, it places my scent all over them and anything they touch. In this way, other animals – especially other cats – know that they are my humans.

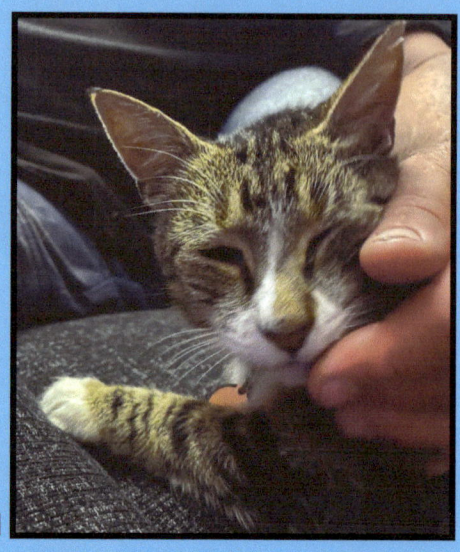

Mum says that I shed loads of hair in those first few weeks. I don't remember much about that, but apparently several pillows could have been stuffed. I'm sure this is one of the reasons people collect our discarded hair so eagerly. People do things that might seem a little odd to us cats. Another one is how they collect our poo from the litter box. What on earth could they possibly want it for? Ewwww…

I soon grew a lovely thick, glossy coat to replace my shabby, neglected one, helped by my new healthy, protein-rich diet and I keep it in tip-top condition by grooming myself thoroughly several times a day. I think you should understand my stance on cleanliness by now! I also undergo regular check-ups with my lovely vet, Dr. Nicola, from First Vets in Whanganui. Good health is very important.

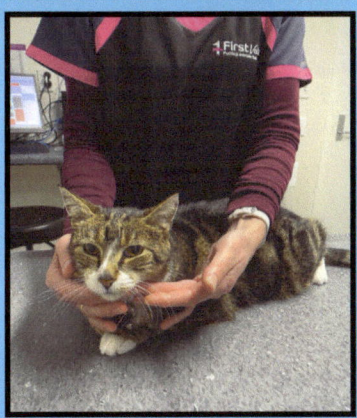

I love my chicken meals. After my encounter with those chickens on the farm during my exile from Marton, I developed an obsession with the way they taste, so Mum and Dad indulge me with my favourite: the occasional delicious treat of deep-fried chicken from the local Four Square. Theirs is the best! Don't worry: my parents are careful and don't give it to me too often!

I have a catio in the corner of the courtyard, surrounded by shrubbery. This is where I like to take the fresh air on days that are warm. From my catio, I can listen to the sounds of the farm which include horses, chickens, ducks and, of course, the goat. Truth be told, my outdoor life is well and truly behind me now. I had more than my fair share of the elements when I was living rough, and far prefer being indoors. Now that I'm a retired pussy cat, I have the luxury of reclining on the comfortable bed I share with Mum and Dad. I spend most of the day snoozing there or sun-puddling in the rays that pour in through the ranch-sliders. I don't mind having them sleep on my bed. In fact, I rather like it when they join me at night and we all cosy up together.

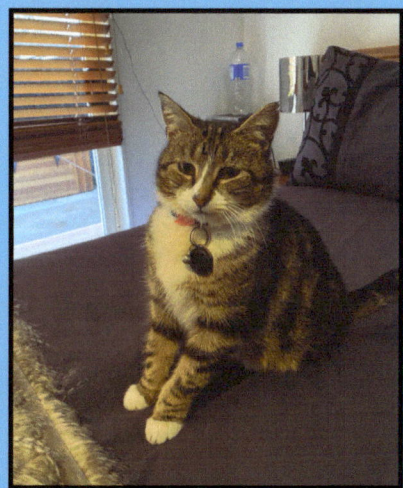

Before we get there, we must have our night-time routine in which I demand fifteen minutes of exercise with my fluffies: a feather stick I love to play with. I do have the option of using several other cat-sized beds and even have my own little electric blanket which I use on

very cold nights, but I seldom spend a full night there – it's so much nicer snuggling up to living hot-water bottles, I think you'd agree.

Every now and then, I feel sad when I remember all the lost and unwanted cats I met. They don't have a home like mine or people to call their own. It is at times like these that I realise how lucky I am, and I just grab Mum and hold her tight. I'm very closely bonded to her and love to cuddle up with her at night. I love Dad too and sometimes cuddle with him, but he's an old-school bloke and I don't want to make him feel uncomfortable, but it's mostly because he's a sound sleeper, my Dad, and I'd hate for him to roll over and squash me in his sleep. He has learned not to wiggle his toes around me, especially in bed, because I WILL pounce on them. I can't help it: they remind me of the times when I had to catch my own food and the instinct kicks in automatically. I am working on it but in the meantime, Dad has to be very careful.

As a token of my appreciation for all they've done for me, I like to wash both of them. They seem incapable of doing it themselves. Sure, they stand under that water splashy thing in the bathroom, but it's not the best way. I've become very good at grooming them. It's quite a challenge getting them to stay still, so I find it best to do it in the middle of the night when they're sound asleep. Mum says there's nothing quite like a sandpaper tongue to wake her up!

I love my "cuddly" which is a woollen blue-checked blankie. I also love my "fluffies". I've had several because I demolish them easily. Mum and Dad have become familiar faces at the local pet store for this reason alone. Stuffed toy mice are another favourite, especially the ones with nip inside. These are all good for my mental and physical health, and they're good for Dad too. Indulging me with a few minutes of play helps keep his toes safe and I can exercise my hunting skills to get rid of pent-up energy at the same time.

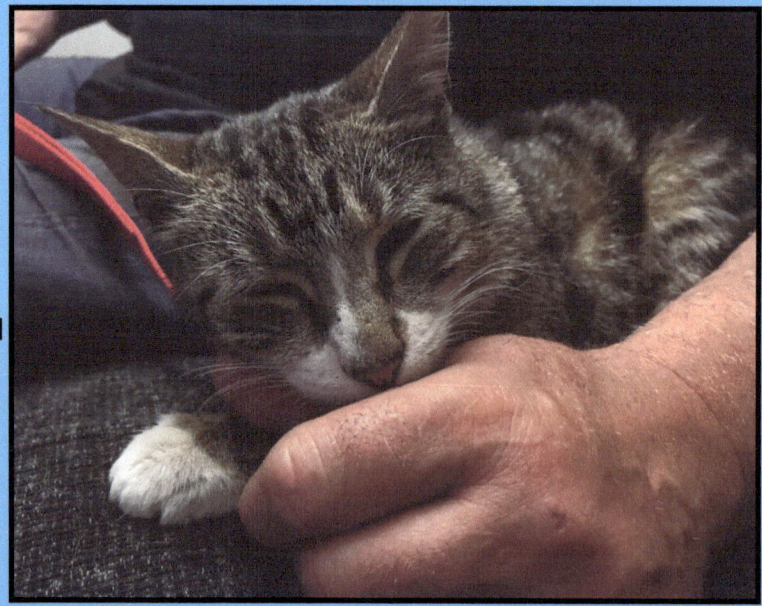

I am Mom and Dad's favourite fur-child, but I do have fur siblings. You can read all about them in my other book: Rodney the Cat - Beyond Lost and Found.

Despite the hardships I had to endure, I am now a very happy cat. From my humble beginnings as a kitten born in the yard of a hardware store, living rough under the pallets, I worked my way up to the role of Chief Pest Control Officer with responsibilities in Public Relations. When I was made unexpectedly redundant, I struck out on my own and survived for many months without a home. I have come a long way to be where I am: comfortably retired. I seem to have become something of a celebrity with followers all over the world. I have (and still do) regularly receive beautiful gifts and treat bags from them, and my list of special Aunties and Uncles continues to grow. My Aunty Viv has even named one of her menu items after me! If you're ever in Sanson, be sure to visit Viv's Kitchen and ask for a **Rodney Slice** with your coffee.

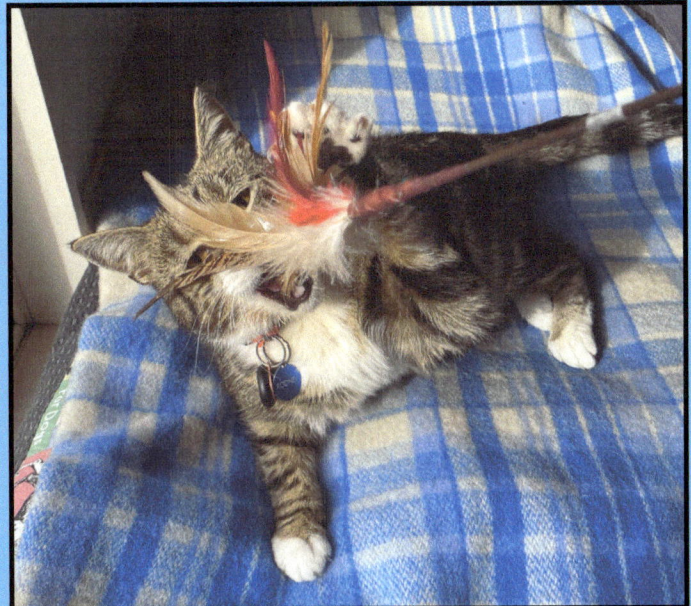

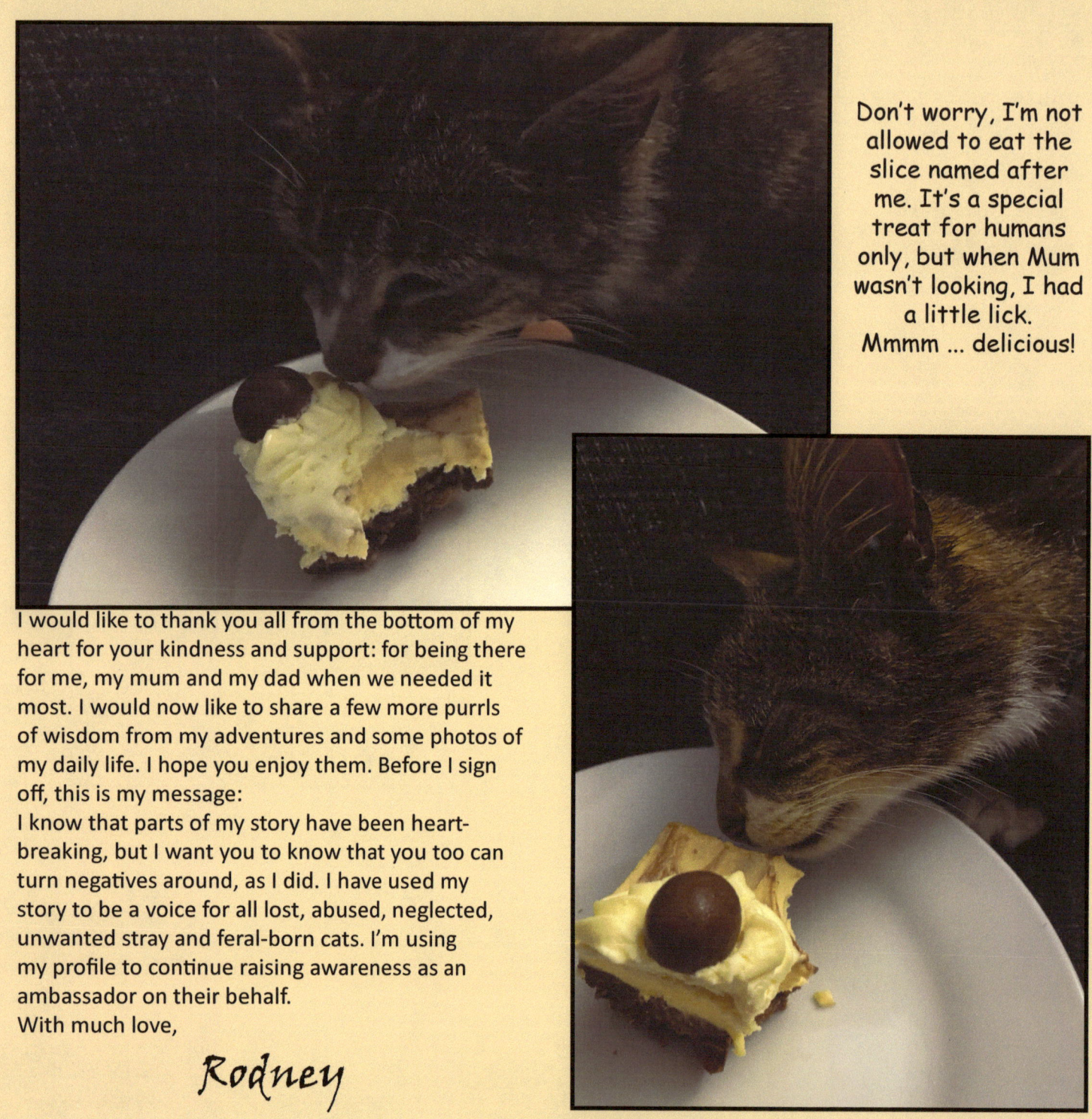

Don't worry, I'm not allowed to eat the slice named after me. It's a special treat for humans only, but when Mum wasn't looking, I had a little lick. Mmmm ... delicious!

I would like to thank you all from the bottom of my heart for your kindness and support: for being there for me, my mum and my dad when we needed it most. I would now like to share a few more purrls of wisdom from my adventures and some photos of my daily life. I hope you enjoy them. Before I sign off, this is my message:

I know that parts of my story have been heart-breaking, but I want you to know that you too can turn negatives around, as I did. I have used my story to be a voice for all lost, abused, neglected, unwanted stray and feral-born cats. I'm using my profile to continue raising awareness as an ambassador on their behalf.

With much love,

Rodney

Hangin' out in my catio.

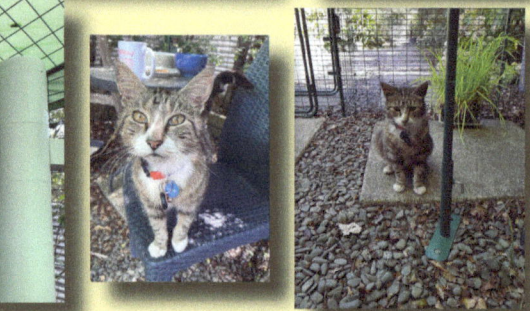

A bit of sun-puddling every day is very good for mental health.

Exercise and rest will also do you the world of good.

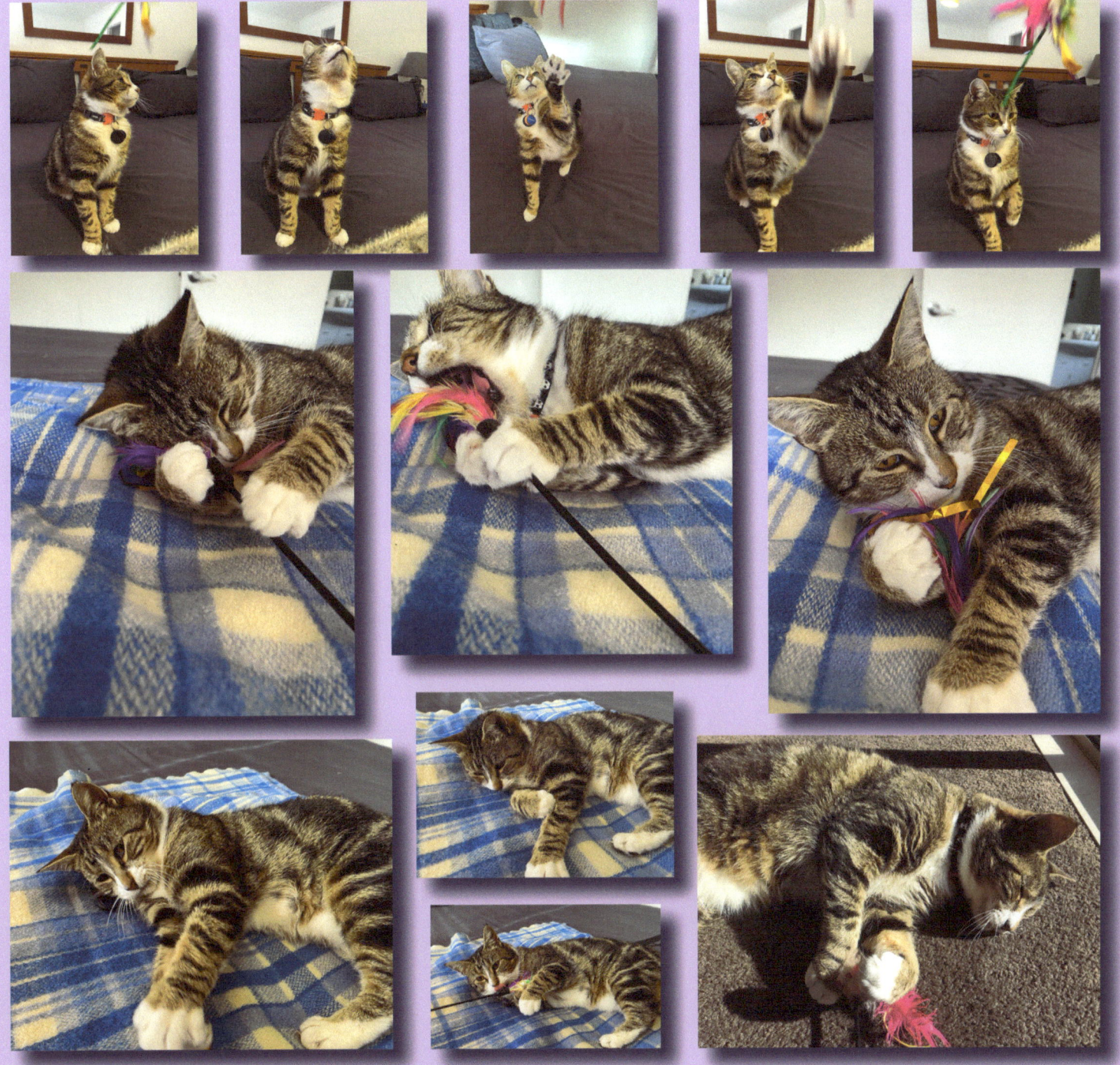

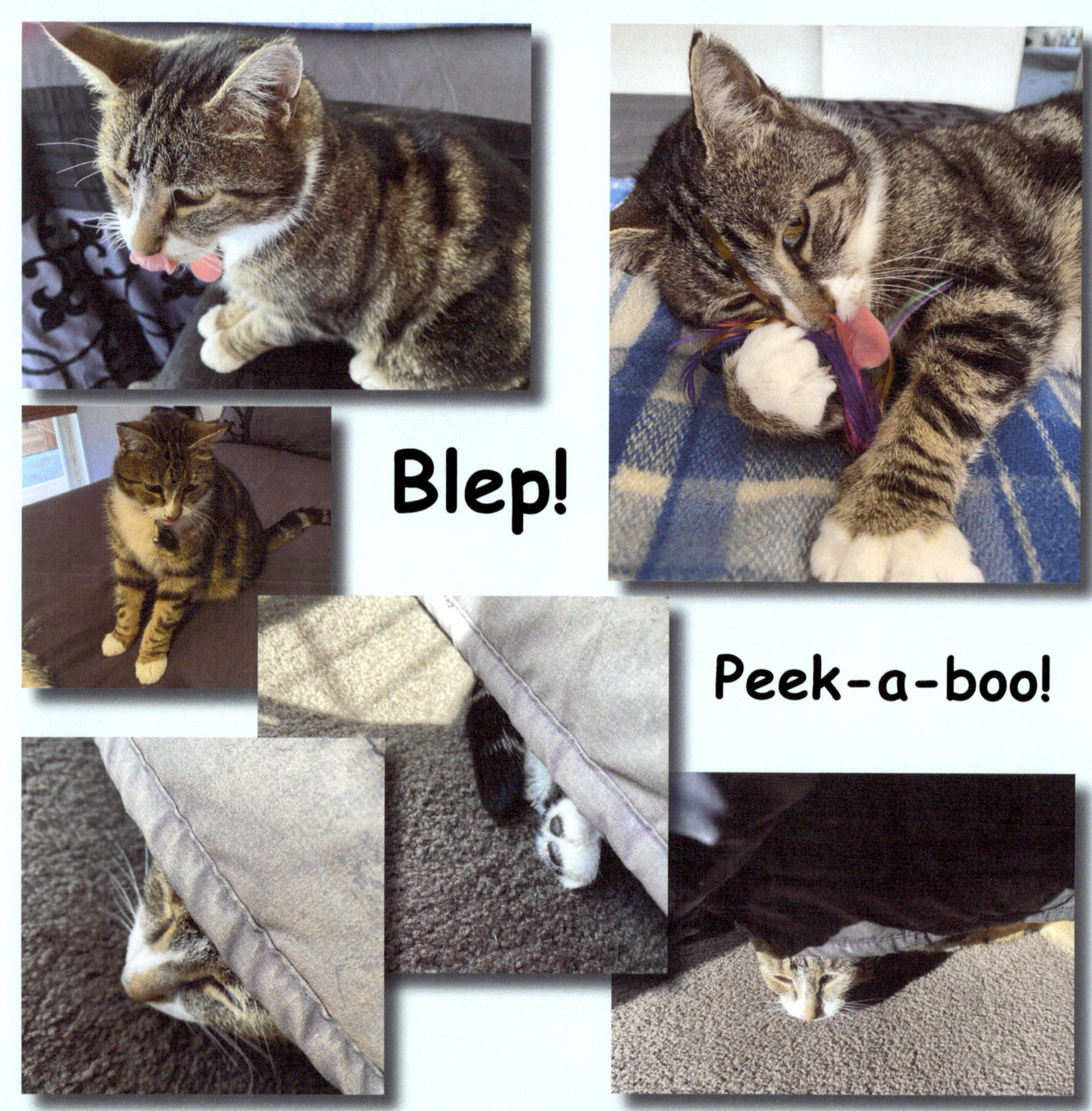

When you do good things for others, it always comes back to you! That's how I met my girl, Gina. Isn't she cute? I pawticipated in a book purroject to raise funds for kitty shelters. You can order a copy of this book too by emailing: cats@deanes.co.nz

Just chillin' with my peeps.

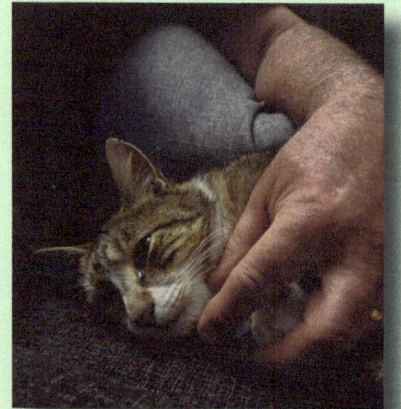

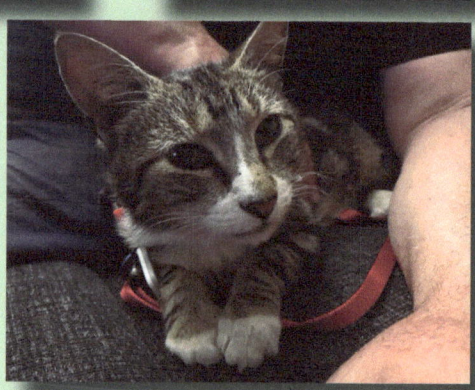

Feral Faces

Take a good look at these photos of abandoned, unwanted, neglected, homeless, stray and feral cats around the world. Any one of them could have been me, fighting for survival. Every single one of these cats is living a hard life as a direct result of human ignorance, selfishness, stupidity or cruelty. My message to humanity is this: please be kind to one another and be kind to animals. If you keep us as pets, please have us spayed or neutered and microchipped and registered. Don't harm us. **You** are the only species with the power to stop the cycle of cruelty.

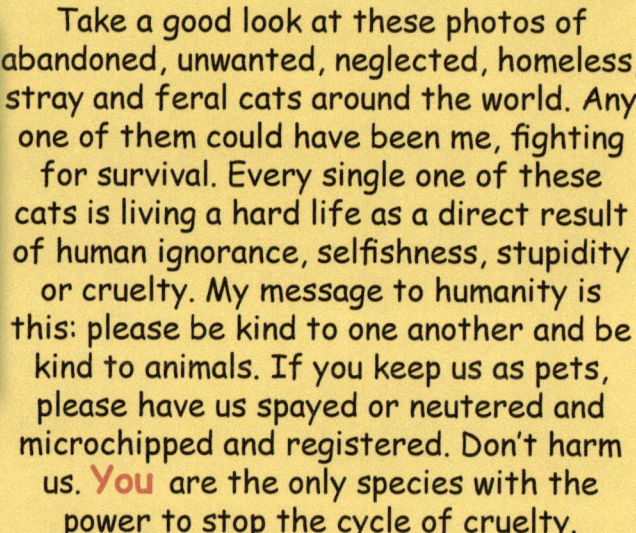

How you treat any creature is the true reflection of your *own* worth.

Forgiveness won't change what happened, but it will change what happens.

Resentment and bitterness are the bars that keep you in your own prison.

R.I.P Rodney

At 2.45PM on Monday, August 14th, 2023, our beloved Rodney crossed the Rainbow Bridge after a short illness.

The story of Rodney the Cat began thirteen years ago. He was born in a hardware and building supply yard in Marton, a country town on the North Island of New Zealand. Graduating from life in the woodpile to a permanent position as resident shop cat, he diligently kept the store free of rats, mice and other pests. The customers loved him, but after ten years of loyal service, he was cruelly taken from his place of employment and dumped in the wild on a chilly, wet morning in the middle of Winter. This is where our role in his story began.

I was devastated at the news of Rodney being dumped and was determined not only to find him, but to bring him home to Shane and me.

Rodney was eventually found with the help of the community, but it didn't end there: rescue politics stood in the way of Rodney being safely homed with us, and he was relocated to New Plymouth where he was lost for a second time. We never gave up. We raised money all over again to get another search underway, deploying state-of-the-art technology purchased with the help of our generous donors. After many days of community effort, Rodney was re-found!

We are deeply grateful for the unwavering love and support you showed throughout Rodney's tumultuous journey. From the time he was dumped in Marton and through two extensive search and rescue operations, your solidarity was our rock. Your presence and support were beyond compare, especially in the distress of his forced relocation and subsequent disappearance in Taranaki. We have no doubt that the power of your positivity brought him finally – and joyously – back to become our boy in Wanganui. His journey was a series of highs and lows, aptly termed the "Rodney Rollercoaster," but your support maintained us throughout. It is something we will eternally cherish.

We will never know exactly what happened to Rodney during his adventures when he was twice lost, but we hope you enjoy this blend of fact and fiction. We've tried to fill in the blanks with a story of what he might very well have experienced. Our dear Rodney epitomised bravery and possessed a heart of gold, refusing to let adversity dampen his affectionate, loving nature. He knew he was enveloped in love, not only from us but from his loyal followers.

His days with us were taken up by his favourite pastime, sun-puddling, and his nights were spent snuggling in Mum and Dad's embrace in the big bed. Rodney brought joy to countless individuals and played an important role in raising awareness about lost, unwanted, and stray animals, both nationally and internationally.

His legacy endures beyond the grave, supporting Animal Rescues with care packages from the proceeds of his merchandise.

Rodney is no longer physically present, but his memory endures. We hear that he has assumed the mantle of Chief Meeter and Greeter at the Rainbow Bridge. We miss him acutely but are comforted by all that he has achieved in his short time on this planet.

Rest in "lurrves", beautiful Rodney, and keep doing good at the Rainbow Bridge. You were first and foremost about love and kindness, and you were the most gentle, loving boy despite all your ordeals and the curveballs of life. If love could have preserved your earthly existence, Rodney, you would have lived forever. This is not a farewell: it's merely a 'see you later'.

Raye and Shane,
Rodney's Mum & Dad

We're most honoured to have been selected as the beneficiary charity for this, the legacy edition of Rodney's book. Thank you for supporting us with your purchase.

Feline Fix is a cat charity with a mission to facilitate and subsidise the spaying and neutering of as many cats as we possibly can. We believe this is the only way to end the cycle of suffering and misery experienced by unwanted cats breeding out of control. We aim to educate people about the benefits of spaying and neutering their cats, and we help out financially when it is unaffordable. To do this, we rely on the generous donations of the community and our various fundraising events. To read more about our work, look us up on Facebook:

facebook.com/ronniesmum2019

I'd like to dedicate this edition of Rodney's story to my beloved husband and companion of nearly 40 years.

Les, you were my anchor. Your sensible, level-headed approach to life kept me grounded in this often-chaotic world of cat rescue. Your sense of humour kept me balanced and reminded me to stop and smell the roses. I miss you more than words can ever express, and I thank you for your unwavering support in my mission to save all cats.

Not many men would have understood the way you did. I trust you've met up with Garfie, Cherry and Charley up there on Planet Cat, and that Rodney is keeping an eye on you all. Ronnie and I are looking forward to the family reunion some day when our work down here too is done.

Your ever-loving wife, Annette
(aka The Cat Fixer)
and your ginger boy Ronnie
(who misses you terribly, especially the long catnaps together on the couch, and "those sneaky snacks when Mom wasn't around to lay down the law and enforce the diet regime").

A Few Final Rainbow Bridge Tributes

Pinky by Patti Cummings

Pinky, the feline companion I rescued, remained a cherished presence in my life for 21 years. Initially frail and a victim of abuse, she transformed into a vibrant and resilient kitty within just three days. Throughout our time together, she faithfully slept by my head, making every moment of those 21 years special.

Cleo by Sue Keats

Last month, I had to bid farewell to my beloved Cleo. She was an extraordinary cat—intelligent, talkative, sweet, and filled with humour. The void left by her absence is deeply felt, and I miss her tremendously.

Madison by Helen Topfer

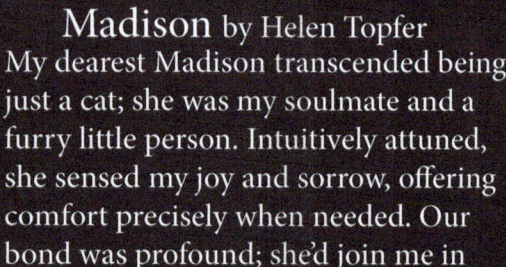

My dearest Madison transcended being just a cat; she was my soulmate and a furry little person. Intuitively attuned, she sensed my joy and sorrow, offering comfort precisely when needed. Our bond was profound; she'd join me in meditation, and a simple glance exchanged between us spoke volumes. Maddy, as affectionate with people as with animals, held a secure place in my heart without a trace of jealousy or grumpiness toward other pets. Our love was boundless and unconditional. Even at the remarkable age of nineteen and a half, when she crossed over the rainbow bridge, Madison left an irreplaceable void in my life. Her memory will forever be cherished, and my love for her knows no bounds.

Tuppence & Bella by Viv Withers

Tuppence graced our lives for 18 years—an exquisitely beautiful soul with a fiercely independent nature. Though she never perched on your knee, her love was unmistakable and profound. Tiny Bella, was a fleeting presence of merely 4 months. Despite her frail health, she proved to be a formidable little fighter. Though small in size, her heart was immense, and she gave so much love in her short life.

Jasmine by Deborah Harvey

After my mom (and hers) passed away, she went through a period of waiting by the door, longing for Mom's return. It took six weeks for her grief to gradually ease. Since she and my mom lived with me, I became her new caregiver. Jasmine was an exceptional cat—dignified yet a bit bossy, even enforcing strict bedtime routines. It was heartbreaking when she passed away at the age of 18. However, six months later, another little Siamese cat unexpectedly entered my life. I can't help but feel that Jasmine must have sent him my way.

Sugar by Gilda Wilkerson

This cherished photograph captures the essence of my beloved and sweet Sugar, making it my favorite. In February of this year, she gracefully crossed over the Rainbow Bridge at the age of 10.

WARNING: The stories that follow contain content that some readers may find upsetting. Discretion is advised.

Tabby & Casper by Jo Day

I have an 11-year-old daughter named Emily who faces several challenges—epilepsy, mild cerebral palsy with a slight weakness on her right side, and significant anxiety stemming from a traumatic incident at school when she was eight.

In response to the distress, we chose to keep Emily at home, where she engages in distance education. Our family included two Oriental Shorthair cats, brother and sister, whom we showed with notable success. Tragedy struck after Casper, the male, won Kitten of the Year in his first year but was then attacked and killed by a neighboring dog. Then Tabytha, our shining star, known as Princess Tabytha for her regal demeanor, won Reserve Cat of the Year in her second year, a period marred by the loss of both Casper and my dear father within a week.

One day, after months of grieving, Tabytha exhibited unusual behavior, frantically leading me to my daughter's room. Emily, having a seizure, had fallen to the floor—an unprecedented occurrence. Tabytha, deeply connected to Emily, seemed to communicate, "You're the mom, you fix her." This was the first time she alerted me to Emily's condition.

Tragically, within a week, Tabytha escaped and met the same fate as Casper, attacked by the neighbor's dog. I heard her scream, rushed to her aid, and she passed away in my arms on the way to the vet.

The pain of losing both cats in the same manner by the same dog was indescribable. Determined to ensure the safety of future pets, we are selling our current home and moving. We've decided not to bring another cat into our lives until we can secure a home that prevents the possibility of our dog inadvertently letting them out—a challenging task in our old Queenslander house. The memories of Casper and Tabytha remain etched in our hearts, and their untimely losses have left an enduring impact on our family.

Puffball, Phoebe and Jasmine by Val Burr

Puffball and Phoebe were littermates and belonged to my daughter, Tanya. Jasmine was Phoebe's kitten and a gift to us from Tanya. Puffball was particularly attached to Tanya and she to him. They missed each other terribly while she was away in Norway for an extended period. Finally, it was time for her to return but then the unthinkable happened. Barely 24 hours after her return home to her flat, my daughter was killed in a brutal home invasion witnessed by her cats. Puffball was particularly traumatised.

We brought them home to join our family of four other cats but things did not go smoothly and the relationships between the cats were rocky at best. However, we made it work. We had no other choice.
In 2016 after his health began to deteriorate rapidly, we let Puffball cross the Rainbow Bridge to be reunited with our (and his) beloved Tanya.
Two years later Phoebe joined them and three years after that, so did Jasmine - the last of Tanya's line of cats. Our hearts have been broken so many times and words cannot adequately express the pain of losing them all.
Pictured here is Tanya and her soulmate, Puffball.

Shera by Lunca Susanna

Allow me to share the touching story of my beloved Shera. She, along with her sister, came from a neighbour known for having cats but neglecting them. Upon discovering another litter of two girls and one boy, born to their young mother at just six months old, I resolved that they wouldn't endure the same fate. When they were seven weeks old, the neighbour approached me, expressing his weariness and the costs involved, prompting me to bring the girls home.

At that time, Misty, a one-year-old cat of mine, immediately embraced Freya as her own, while Shera formed a special bond with me. Wherever I went, she was by my side, sleeping on me and remaining close. In the week leading up to December 22, 2020, she became even more affectionate than usual.

On that fateful morning, as we all gathered for breakfast, Shera suddenly stood up from my chest, booped my nose, leaped off the bed, emitted an unusual sound, and collapsed—her passing accompanied by a sound forever etched in my memory. I chose to have her cremated, a tradition I followed for all my feline companions.

In March of the following year, I fell seriously ill, and specialists warned that waiting any longer would have resulted in my demise. Transported to a hospital in Belgium, I faced additional challenges, including harassment by a male nurse. One day, feeling a comforting presence, I looked at the sink and sensed Shera and the little black Bakira, another rescue of mine. I spoke to Shera, asking her to be my guardian and prevent me from falling asleep to thwart any potential molestation from the predator. Despite dozing off, a sudden loud noise startled everyone, including the other nurses, who couldn't determine its source. Grateful for Shera's protective presence, I made a promise that if I survived, I would get a tattoo in her honour, along with the other girls I had lost.

True to my word, I now bear a tattoo of Shera looking around the corner, accompanied by three stars representing the ones I have lost. While Shera may no longer be with us, her sister Freya, aged 15, and Misty, aged 16, continue to share my life, along with the two three-year-old sisters, Bakira and Bonita. Thank you for allowing me to share the memories of my beloved pets with you.

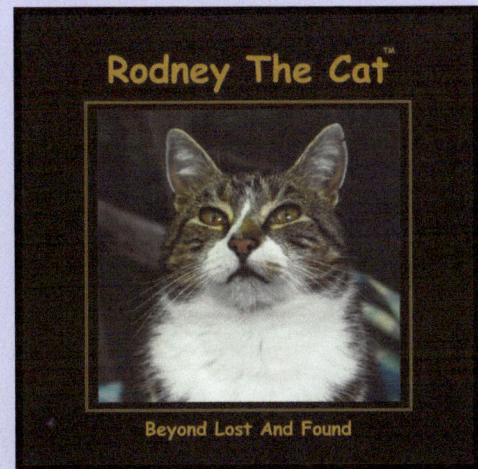

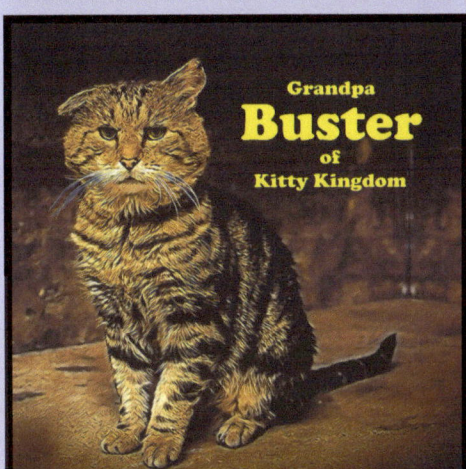

I hope you've enjoyed Rodney's story. To order any of my other books, email:

cats@deanes.co.nz

Linda Deane
The Not-So-Crazy Cat Lady©

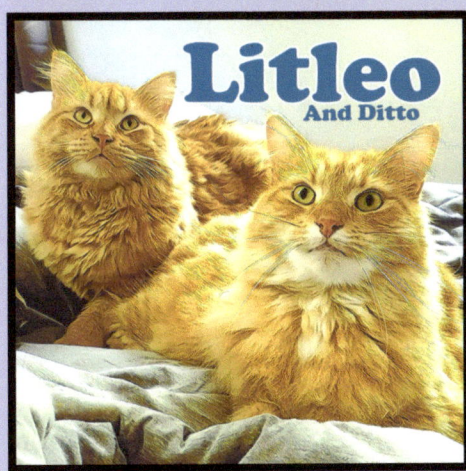

www.ingramcontent.com/pod-product-compliance
Lightning Source LLC
Chambersburg PA
CBHW042246100526
44587CB00002B/42